Introduction to React

Cory Gackenheimer

Apress®

Introduction to React

ISBN-13 (pbk): 978-1-4842-1246-2

ISBN-13 (electronic): 978-1-4842-1245-5

Managing Director: Welmoed Spahr
Lead Editor: Louise Corrigan
Technical Reviewer: Akshat Paul
Editorial Board: Steve Anglin, Mark Beckner, Gary Cornell, Louise Corrigan, James DeWolf, Jonathan Gennick, Robert Hutchinson, Michelle Lowman, James Markham, Matthew Moodie, Jeffrey Pepper, Douglas Pundick, Ben Renow-Clarke, Gwenan Spearing, Matt Wade, Steve Weiss
Coordinating Editor: Kevin Walter
Copy Editor: Kezia Endsley
Compositor: SPi Global
Indexer: SPi Global
Artist: SPi Global
Cover Designer: Crest

Distributed to the book trade worldwide by Springer Science+Business Media New York, 233 Spring Street, 6th Floor, New York, NY 10013. Phone 1-800-SPRINGER, fax (201) 348-4505, e-mail orders-ny@springer-sbm.com, or visit www.springeronline.com. Apress Media, LLC is a California LLC and the sole member (owner) is Springer Science + Business Media Finance Inc (SSBM Finance Inc). SSBM Finance Inc is a Delaware corporation.

For information on translations, please e-mail rights@apress.com, or visit www.apress.com.

Apress and friends of ED books may be purchased in bulk for academic, corporate, or promotional use. eBook versions and licenses are also available for most titles. For more information, reference our Special Bulk Sales–eBook Licensing web page at www.apress.com/bulk-sales.

Any source code or other supplementary material referenced by the author in this text is available to readers at www.apress.com. For detailed information about how to locate your book's source code, go to www.apress.com/source-code/.

For my kids and their mother.

Contents at a Glance

Contents

About the Author

Cory Gackenheimer is a software engineer from the Midwest. He studied physics at Purdue University, where he worked with image analysis software for nanoscale environments. His software experience has led him to utilize a wide variety of technologies, including JavaScript. He is a member of the jQuery Mobile Team and regularly contributes to open source projects. In his spare time, he enjoys working on Node.js-based projects and incorporating React into his projects.

About the Technical Reviewer

Akshat Paul is a developer and author of the book *RubyMotion iOS Development Essentials*. He has extensive experience in mobile and web development and has delivered many enterprise and consumer applications over the years.

In other avatars, Akshat frequently speaks at conferences and meetups on various technologies. He has given talks at RubyConfIndia and #inspect-RubyMotion Conference, Brussels and was the keynote speaker at Technology Leadership Events at bkk & kl. Besides writing code, Akshat spends time with his family, is an avid reader, and is obsessive about healthy eating.

Acknowledgments

This book would not have happened without a call from an amazing editor, Louise Corrigan, whose enthusiasm for me to write another book was irresistible. I also have to acknowledge my family, who tolerated time spent away from them while I researched, coded, and wrote this book. Without their patience, I would not have been able to finish. Finally, thanks to you, the reader, whose interest in React has led you here to begin your React journey. Enjoy!

CHAPTER 1

■ ■ ■

What Is React?

It gives me great pleasure indeed to see the stubbornness of an incorrigible nonconformist warmly acclaimed.

—Albert Einstein

You may have picked up this book with some level of JavaScript knowledge. There is also a high probability that you have an idea of what React is. This chapter highlights the key aspects of React as a framework, explains the problems it solves, and describes how you can utilize the features and the rest of the information contained in this book to better your web development practices and create complex, yet maintainable user interfaces using React.

Defining React

React is a JavaScript framework. React was originally created by engineers at Facebook to solve the challenges involved when developing complex user interfaces with datasets that change over time. This is not a trivial undertaking and must not only be maintainable, but also scalable to work at the scale of Facebook. React was actually born in Facebook's ads organization, where they had been utilizing a traditional client-side Model-View-Controller approach. Applications such as these normally consist of two-way data binding along with rendering template. React changed the way that these applications were created by making some daring advances in web development. When React was released in 2013, the web development community was both interested and seemingly disgusted by what React was doing.

As you will discover throughout this book, React challenges conventions that have become the de-facto standards for JavaScript framework best practices. React does this by introducing many new paradigms and shifting the status quo of what it takes to create scalable and maintainable JavaScript applications and user interfaces. Along with the shift in front-end development mentality, React comes with a rich set of features that make composing a single-page application or user interface approachable for developers of many skill levels—from those who have just been introduced to JavaScript, to seasoned veterans of the web. You will see these features—such as the virtual DOM, JSX, and Flux concepts—as you read this book and discover how they can be used to create complex user interfaces.

You will also see, in brief, how Facebook is continually challenging the development world with React Native. React Native is a new open source library for creating native user interfaces utilizing the same principles as React's JavaScript library. By creating a Native UI library, React has pushed its value proposition of "learn once, write anywhere." This paradigm shift applies to being able to utilize the core concepts of React in order to make maintainable interfaces. By now it is possible you are thinking that there is nothing React can't do when it comes to development. This is not the case, and in order to further understand what React is, you need an understanding of what React is *not*, which you learn later in this chapter. First, you will understand the underlying problems that caused React to be created and how React solves those problems.

Why React?

As already noted, React is a different concept when it comes to web development in general. It is a shift from generally accepted workflows and best practices. Why is it that Facebook shirked these trends in favor of creating an entirely new vision of the web development process? Was it just extremely cavalier to challenge accepted best practices, or was there a generalized business case for creating React?

If you look at the reasoning behind React, you'll see that it was a created to fill a specific need for a specific set of technological challenges faced by Facebook. These challenges were and are not unique to Facebook, but what Facebook did was tackle the challenges directly with an approach to solve the problem by itself. You could think of this as an analogue of the Unix philosophy summarized by Eric Raymond in his book, *The Art of Unix Programming*. In the book, Raymond writes about the Rule of Modularity, which reads,

> *The only way to write complex software that won't fall on its face is to hold its global complexity down—to build it out of simple parts connected by well-defined interfaces—so that most problems are local and you can have some hope of upgrading a part without breaking the whole.*

This is precisely the approach that React takes in solving the troubles of complex user interfaces. Facebook, when developing React, did not create a full Model-View-Controller architecture to supplant existing frameworks. There was not a need to reinvent that particular wheel and add complexity to the problem of creating large-scale user interfaces. React was created to solve a singular problem.

React was built to deal with displaying data in a user interface. You might think that displaying data in a user interface is a problem that's already been solved, and you would be correct in thinking that way. The difference is that React was created to serve large-scale user interfaces—Facebook and Instagram scale interfaces—with data that changes over time. This sort of interface can be created and solved with tools that exist outside of React. In fact, Facebook must have solved these issues before it created React. But Facebook did create React because it had valid reasoning and found that React can be used to solve specific problems encountered when building complex user interfaces.

What Problems Does React Solve?

React does not set out to solve every problem that you will encounter in user interface design and front-end development. React solves a specific set of problems, and in general, a single problem. As stated by Facebook and Instagram, React builds large-scale user interfaces with data that changes over time.

Large-scale user interfaces with data that changes over time could probably be something that many web developers can relate to in their own work or hobby coding experiences. In the modern web development world, you often offload much of the responsibility of the user interface to the browser and HTML, CSS, and JavaScript. These types of applications are commonly referred to as single page applications, where the common request/response to the server is limited to showcase the power of the browser. This is natural; why would you not do this, since most browsers are capable of doing complex layout and interaction?

The problem arises when your weekend project code is no longer maintainable. You have to "bolt on" extra pieces of code to get the data to bind properly. Sometimes you have to restructure an application because a secondary business requirement has inadvertently broken the way the interface renders a few interactions after the user starts a task. All of this leads to user interfaces that are fragile, highly interconnected, and not easily maintainable. These are all problems that React attempts to solve.

Take for example the client-side Model-View-Controller architecture with two-way data binding in templates you saw mentioned earlier. This application must contain views that listen to models, and then the views independently update their presentation based on either user interaction or the model changing. In a basic application this is not a noticeable bottleneck for performance, or more importantly, for developer productivity. The scale of this application will inevitably grow as new models and views are added to the application. These are all connected through a delicate and intricate mess of code that can direct the relations of each of the views and their models. This quickly becomes more and more complicated. Items that live deep in the rendering chain or in a far away model are now affecting the output of other items. In many cases an update that happens may not even be fully knowable by the developer because maintaining a tracking mechanism becomes increasingly difficult. This makes developing and testing your code harder, which means that it becomes harder to develop a method or new feature and release it. The code is now less predictable and development time has skyrocketed. This is exactly the problem that React sets out to solve.

At first React was a thought experiment. Facebook thought that they had already written the initial layout code to describe what the application could and should look like, so why not just run the startup code again when the data or state changes the application? You likely are cringing right now because you know that this means they would be sacrificing performance and user experience. When you completely replace code in a browser, you are going to see flickers of the screen and flashes of unstyled content. It will just appear to be inefficient. Facebook knew this, but also noted that what it did create—a mechanism for replacing the state when data changes—was actually working to some degree. Facebook then decided that if the replace mechanism could be optimized, it would have a solution. This is how React was born as the solution to a specific set of problems.

3

React Is Not Just Another Framework

In many cases when you learn something, you first need to realize what the thing is that you are learning. In the case of React, it can be helpful to learn which concepts are not parts of the React framework. This will help you understand which standard practices you have learned need to be unlearned, or at least need to be set aside, in order to fully understand the concepts of a new framework such as React. So what is it that makes React different and why is it important?

Many argue that React is a full-scale JavaScript framework on a level that compares to other frameworks such as Backbone, Knockout.js, AngularJS, Ember, CanJS, Dojo, or any of the numerous MVC frameworks that exist. Figure 1-1 shows an example of a typical MVC framework.

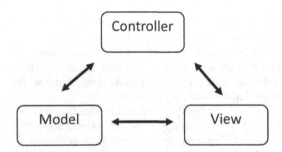

Figure 1-1. *A basic MVC architecture*

Figure 1-1 shows the basics of each of the components in a Model-View-Controller architecture. The model handles the state of the application and sends state-changing events to the view. The view is the user-facing look and interaction interface to the end user. The view can send events to the controller, and in some cases to the model. The controller is the main dispatcher of events, which can be sent to the model, to update state, and the view to update the presentation. You may note that this is a generic representation of what an MVC architecture is, and in reality there are so many variants and customized implementations that there is no single MVC architecture. The point isn't to state what an MVC structure looks like, but to point out what React is not.

This MVC structure is actually not a fair assessment of what React is or intends to be. That is because React is one particular piece of what these frameworks present. React is in its simplest form, just the view of these MVC, MVVM, or MV* frameworks. As you saw in the previous section, React is a way to describe the user interface of an application and a mechanism to change that over time as data changes. React is made with declarative components that describe an interface. React uses no observable data binding when building an application. React is also easy to manipulate, because you can take the components you create and combine them to make custom components that work as you expect every time because it can scale. React can scale better than other frameworks because of the principles that drove it from its creation. When creating React interfaces, you structure them in such as way that they are built out of multiple components.

Let's pause for a minute and examine the most basic structure of several frameworks and then compare them to React in order to highlight the differences. For each of the frameworks, you will examine the most basic to-do list applications as they are created for the http://todomvc.com web site. I am not going to deride other frameworks because they all serve a purpose. Instead I attempt to demonstrate how React is structured compared to the others. I showcase just the important parts to highlight and limit a complete recreation of the application here. If you want to see the full examples, the links to the source are included. Try not to become too focused on the implementation details of any of these examples, including the React example, because as you progress through this book the concepts will be covered thoroughly and will help you understand what is going on completely.

Ember.js

Ember.js is a popular framework that utilizes a MVC framework composed of views in the form of handlebars templates. In this section, note that there is a bit of work to do in order to facilitate the integration of the templates, models, and controllers. This is not to say that Ember.js is a bad framework, because modification is a byproduct of such a framework.

In Listing 1-1, which is the body of the TodoMVC Ember.js example, you see that the markup consists of two handlebars templates for the to-do list and the to-dos.

Listing 1-1. Body of TodoMVC with Ember.js

```
<body>
    <script type="text/x-handlebars" data-template-name="todo-list">
    /* Handlebars todo-list template */
    </script>
    <script type="text/x-handlebars" data-template-name="todos">
    /* Handlebars todos template */
    </script>
    <script src="node_modules/todomvc-common/base.js"></script>
    <script src="node_modules/jquery/dist/jquery.js"></script>
    <script src="node_modules/handlebars/dist/handlebars.js"></script>
    <script src="node_modules/components-ember/ember.js"></script>
    <script src="node_modules/ember-data/ember-data.js"></script>
    <script src="node_modules/ember-localstorage-adapter/localstorage_
                adapter.js"></script>
    <script src="js/app.js"></script>
    <script src="js/router.js"></script>
    <script src="js/models/todo.js"></script>
    <script src="js/controllers/todos_controller.js"></script>
    <script src="js/controllers/todos_list_controller.js"></script>
    <script src="js/controllers/todo_controller.js"></script>
    <script src="js/views/todo_input_component.js"></script>
    <script src="js/helpers/pluralize.js"></script>
</body>
```

Along with these there are three controllers—an app.js entry point, a router, and a todo input view component. That seems like a lot of files, but in a production environment, that would be minimized. Note the separation of the controllers and views. The views, including the to-do list view shown in Listing 1-2, are quite verbose and make it easy to determine what the code does.

Listing 1-2. Ember.js Handlebars Template

```
{{#if length}}
  <section id="main">
    {{#if canToggle}}
      {{input type="checkbox" id="toggle-all" checked=allTodos.allAreDone}}
    {{/if}}
    <ul id="todo-list">
      {{#each}}
        <li {{bind-attr class="isCompleted:completed isEditing:editing"}}>
          {{#if isEditing}}
            {{todo-input
                type="text"
                class="edit"
                value=bufferedTitle
                focus-out="doneEditing"
                insert-newline="doneEditing"
                escape-press="cancelEditing"}}
          {{else}}
            {{input type="checkbox" class="toggle" checked=isCompleted}}
            <label {{action "editTodo" on="doubleClick"}}>{{title}}</label>
            <button {{action "removeTodo"}} class="destroy"></button>
          {{/if}}
        </li>
      {{/each}}
    </ul>
  </section>
{{/if}}
```

This is a clear example and works as a readable view. There are several properties that are dictated from the controller as you would expect. The controller is named in the router.js file, which also names the view to be used. This controller is shown in the Listing 1-3.

Listing 1-3. Ember.js TodosListController

```
(function () {
    'use strict';

    Todos.TodosListController = Ember.ArrayController.extend({
        needs: ['todos'],
        allTodos: Ember.computed.alias('controllers.todos'),
```

```
            itemController: 'todo',
            canToggle: function () {
                    var anyTodos = this.get('allTodos.length');
                    var isEditing = this.isAny('isEditing');

                    return anyTodos && !isEditing;
            }.property('allTodos.length', '@each.isEditing')
        });
})();
```

You can see that this `TodosListController` takes a model of to-dos and adds some properties along with the `itemController` of `'todo'`. This `todo` controller is actually where most of the JavaScript resides that dictates the actions and conditionals that are visible in the view you saw earlier in this section. As someone who is familiar with Ember. js, this is a well defined and organized example of what Ember.js can do. It is however quite different than React, which you will see soon enough. First, let's examine a bit of the AngularJS TodoMVC example.

AngularJS

AngularJS is perhaps the world's most popular MV* framework. It is extremely simple to get started and has the backing of Google along with many developers who have jumped in and created great tutorials, books, and blog posts. It is of course not the same framework as React, which you will soon see. Listing 1-4 shows the AngularJS TodoMVC application.

Listing 1-4. AngularJS Body

```
<body ng-app="todomvc">
  <ng-view />
    <script type="text/ng-template" id="todomvc-index.html">
      <section id="todoapp">
        <header id="header">
          <h1>todos</h1>
            <form id="todo-form" ng-submit="addTodo()">
              <input
                id="new-todo"
                placeholder="What needs to be done?"
                ng-model="newTodo"
                ng-disabled="saving" autofocus
              >
            </form>
        </header>
        <section id="main" ng-show="todos.length" ng-cloak>
          <input id="toggle-all" type="checkbox" ng-model="allChecked"
          ng-click="markAll(allChecked)">
```

```
            <label for="toggle-all">Mark all as complete</label>
            <ul id="todo-list">
              <li ng-repeat="todo in todos | filter:statusFilter track by $index"
                ng-class="{
                        completed: todo.completed,
                        editing: todo == editedTodo}"
              >
            <div class="view">
              <input class="toggle" type="checkbox" ng-model="todo.completed"
              ng-change="toggleCompleted(todo)">
              <label ng-dblclick="editTodo(todo)">{{todo.title}}</label>
              <button class="destroy" ng-click="removeTodo(todo)"></button>
            </div>
            <form ng-submit="saveEdits(todo, 'submit')">
              <input class="edit" ng-trim="false" ng-model="todo.title"
              todo-escape="revertEdits(todo)" ng-blur="saveEdits(todo, 'blur')"
              todo-focus="todo == editedTodo">
            </form>
            </li>
          </ul>
      </section>
    <footer id="footer" ng-show="todos.length" ng-cloak>
        /* footer template */
    </footer>
</section>
</script>
<script src="node_modules/todomvc-common/base.js"></script>
<script src="node_modules/angular/angular.js"></script>
<script src="node_modules/angular-route/angular-route.js"></script>
<script src="js/app.js"></script>
<script src="js/controllers/todoCtrl.js"></script>
<script src="js/services/todoStorage.js"></script>
<script src="js/directives/todoFocus.js"></script>
<script src="js/directives/todoEscape.js"></script>
</body>
```

You can see already that compared to Ember.js, Angular is more declarative in nature in its templating. You can also see that there are concepts like controllers, directives, and services that are tied to this application. The todoCtrl file holds the controller values that power this view. The next example, shown in Listing 1-5, is just a snippet of this file, but you can see how it works.

Listing 1-5. Todo Controller for AngularJS

```
angular.module('todomvc')
  .controller('TodoCtrl', function TodoCtrl($scope, $routeParams, $filter,
  store) {
  /* omitted */
  $scope.addTodo = function () {
    var newTodo = {
      title: $scope.newTodo.trim(),
      completed: false
    };

    if (!newTodo.title) {
      return;
    }

    $scope.saving = true;
    store.insert(newTodo)
      .then(function success() {
        $scope.newTodo = '';
      })
      .finally(function () {
        $scope.saving = false;
      });
  };
  /* omitted */

});
```

This example showcases the todoCtrl and shows how it builds a $scope mechanism that then allows you to attach methods and properties to your AngularJS view. The next section dives into React and explains how it acts on a user interface in a different way than Ember.js and AngularJS do.

React

As you saw in the other examples, there is a basic structure to the TodoMVC applications that makes them an easy choice for demonstrating differences. Ember.js and AngularJS are two popular frameworks that I think help demonstrate that React is not an MV* framework and just a basic JavaScript framework for building user interfaces. This section details the React example and shows you how to structure a React app from the component level, and then works backward to explain how the components are composed. And now, many pages into a book about React, you finally get to see React code in Listing 1-6.

■ **Note** The code provided is to be run from a web server. This can be a SimpleHTTPServer in Python, an Apache server, or anything else you are accustomed to. If this is not available, you can serve the HTML file in your browser, but you will need to ensure that the files associated are local and can be fetched by your web browser.

Listing 1-6. The Basic HTML of the React Todo App

```
<!-- some lines removed for brevity -->
<body>
    <section id="todoapp"></section>

    <script src="react.js"></script>
    <script src="JSXTransformer.js"></script>
    <script src="js/utils.js"></script>
    <script src="js/todoModel.js"></script>
    <script type="text/jsx" src="js/todoItem.jsx"></script>
    <script type="text/jsx" src="js/footer.jsx"></script>
    <script type="text/jsx" src="js/app.jsx"></script>
</body>
```

In Listing 1-6, you see the body of the basic React todoMVC application. Take note of the section and its id attribute. Compare this body to the AngularJS and Ember.js examples and note that the number of script tags, and therefore files you need to deal with, is dramatically smaller for this type of application. One could argue that the number of files isn't a fair comparison because you could, theoretically, structure an AngularJS application to contain more than just one controller per file, or find similar ways to limit the number of script elements. The point is that React seems to naturally split into these types of structures because of the way that the components are authored. This does not mean that React is definitively better, or even more concise, but that the paradigms that React creates make creating components at the very least seem more concise.

This section will be the target for placing the React components as they are rendered. The scripts that are included are the React library and the JSX transformer file. The next two items are the data models and utilities that are incorporated into every todoMVC application. What follows those items are three JSX files, which comprise the entirety of the application. The application is rendered from a component contained in the app.jsx file, which you will examine in Listing 1-7.

Listing 1-7. app.jsx Render Function

```
var model = new app.TodoModel('react-todos');

function render() {
    React.render(
        <TodoApp model={model}/>,
        document.getElementById('todoapp')
    );
}

model.subscribe(render);
render();
```

Listing 1-7 shows an interesting view of how React works. You will learn how this is implemented in the rest of the book, but the basics are in bold in the example. First, you see what looks like an HTML or XML element <TodoApp model={model}/>. This is the JSX, or the JavaScript XML transpiler, that was created to integrate with React. JSX is not required to be utilized with React, but can make authoring applications much easier. It not only makes writing your React applications easier, but it allows for a more clear syntax when you are reading and updating your code. The previous JSX transforms into a JavaScript function that looks like this:

```
React.createElement(TodoApp, {model: model});
```

This is interesting to note for now, and you will read more about JSX and how it transforms in Chapter 3.

The take-away from this example is that you can create a component and then attach it to the DOM by naming the element in the DOM where you want to attach it as the second argument of the render method. This named element in the previous example was document.getElementById('todoapp'). In the next few examples you will see how the TodoApp component is created and read about the basic ideas that represent how React components are composed, all of which are covered in detail later in the book.

```
var TodoApp = React.createClass({
    /* several methods omitted for brevity */
    render: function() {
        /* see next example */
    }
});
```

From this example, you can see a few core concepts of the composition of this TodoApp component. It first is created using a function called React.createClass(). This function accepts an object. The createClass method will be covered in depth in the following chapter, along with how to author such a component using ES6 classes. Within this object there are several methods in the TodoMVC application, but in this example it is important to highlight the render method, which is required for all React components. You will examine them more closely in Listing 1-8. This is a large method because it handles quite a large portion of what React does, so be patient as you read through it.

Listing 1-8. React TodoMVC Render Method

```
render: function() {
  var footer;
  var main;
  var todos = this.props.model.todos;

  var showTodos = todos.filter(function (todo) {
    switch (this.state.nowShowing) {
    case app.ACTIVE_TODOS:
      return !todo.completed;
    case app.COMPLETED_TODOS:
      return todo.completed;
    default:
      return true;
  }, this);

  var todoItems = shownTodos.map(function (todo) {
    return (
      <TodoItem
        key={todo.id}
        todo={todo}
        onToggle={this.toggle.bind(this, todo)}
        onDestroy={this.destroy.bind(this, todo)}
        onEdit={this.edit.bind(this, todo)}
        editing={this.stat.editing === todo.id}
        onSave={this.save.bind(this, todo)}
        onCancel={this.cancel}
      />
    );
  }, this);

  var activeTodoCount = todos.reduce(function (accum, todo) {
    return todo.completed ? accum : accum + 1;
  }, 0);

  var completedCount = todos.length - activeTodoCount;

  if (activeTodoCount || completedCount) {
    footer =
      <TodoFooter
        count={activeTodoCount}
        completedCount={completedCount}
        nowShowing={this.state.nowShowing}
        onClearCompleted={this.clearCompleted}
      />;
  }
```

```
    if (todos.length) {
      main = (
        <section id="main">
          <input
            id="toggle-all"
            type="checkbox"
            onChange={this.toggleAll}
            checked={activeTodoCount === 0}
          />
          <ul id="todo-list">
            {todoItems}
          </ul>
      );
    }

    return (
      <div>
        <header id="header">
          <h1>todos</h1>
          <input
            ref="newField"
            id="new-todo"
            placeholder="What needs to be done?"
            onKeyDown={this.handleNewTodoKeyDown}
            autoFocus={true}
          />
        </header>
        {main}
        {footer}
      </div>
    );
}
```

As you can see, there is a lot going on here, but what I hope you also see is how simple and declarative this is from a development standpoint. It shows how React is much more declarative than other frameworks, including the AngularJS example. This declarative approach shows exactly what it is that you will be seeing on your page as your application is rendered.

Let's rewind to the beginning of this section, where you saw the <TodoApp model={model} /> component. This component acts as the main component of the render function that was at the end of the app.jsx file. In the most recent example, I bolded some key points in the code. First, note that model={model} is passed into the function and then appears to be addressed as this.props.model.todos, at the beginning of the TodoApp class. This is part of the declarative nature of React. You can declare properties on a component and utilize them in the this.props object within the methods on your component.

13

Next is the concept of subcomponents. The variable todoItems created and referencing another React component called <TodoItem/>. TodoItem is another React component that is created in its own JSX file. Having a TodoItem component that specifically describes the behavior of the specific TodoItems, and having it available as a named element within the TodoApp component, is an incredibly powerful concept. As you build more and more complex applications with React, you will find that knowing precisely what component you need to alter, and that it is isolated and self-contained, will grant you a great deal of confidence in your application's stability. Listing 1-9 is the render function from the TodoItems, component in its entirety.

Listing 1-9. TodoItems Render Method

```
app.TodoItem = React.createClass({
/* omitted code for brevity */

  render: function () {
    return (
        <li className={React.addons.classSet({
            completed: this.props.todo.completed,
            editing: this.props.editing
        })}>
            <div className="view">
                <input
                    className="toggle"
                    type="checkbox"                    •
                    checked={this.props.todo.completed}
                    onChange={this.props.onToggle}
                 />
                <label onDoubleClick={this.handleEdit}>
                    {this.props.todo.title}
                </label>
                <button className="destroy" onClick={this.props.onDestroy} />
            </div>
            <input
                ref="editField"
                className="edit"
                value={this.state.editText}
                onBlur={this.handleSubmit}
                onChange={this.handleChange}
                onKeyDown={this.handleKeyDown}
             />
        </li>
    );
  }
});
```

In this example, you see the rendering of the TodoItem component, which is a subcomponent of the TodoApp. This is simply a component that handles the individual list items that are contained in the TodoApp. This is split off into its own component because it represents its own set of interactions in the application. It can handle editing as well as marking if the item is completed or not. Since this functionality doesn't necessarily need to know or interact with the rest of the application, it is built as a standalone component. It may have been just as easy to add to the TodoApp itself initially, but in the world of React, as you will see later, it is often better to make things more modular. This is because in the future the maintenance costs will be recouped by utilizing this logical separation of interactions.

Now you understand at a high level how interactions can often be contained in subcomponents in a React application. The code of the TodoApp render function shows that the TodoItem exists as a subcomponent and shows that the TodoFooter, contained in a JSX by itself, houses its own interactions. The next important concept is to focus on how these subcomponents are reassembled. The TodoItems are added to an unordered list that is contained in a variable called main, which returns the JSX markup for the main section of the TodoApp. Similarly the footer variable contains the TodoFooter component. These two variables, footer and main, are added to the return value of the TodoApp, which you see at the end of the example. These variables are accessed in JSX by using curly braces so you see them as follows:

```
{main}
{footer}
```

You now have the whole picture, albeit a basic overview, of how React applications and components are built. You can also compare these ideas to the overview of the same application built with Ember.js and Angular, or with any other framework, by visiting todomvc.com. React differs greatly as a framework from the others because it is simply a way to utilize JavaScript to craft complex user interfaces. This means that the interactions are all contained in declarative components. There are no direct observables used to create data binding like other frameworks. The markup is, or at least can be, generated utilizing the embedded XML syntax JSX. And finally you can put all this together to create custom components such as the singular <TodoApp />.

React Concepts and Terminology

This section highlights some of the key terminology and concepts that you will see throughout this book and helps you to understand more clearly what is written in the following chapters. You also get a list of tools and utilities that will help you become comfortable with React right away, from the tools up. Chapter 2 explains in-depth many of the concepts from the React core and progresses into building a React application and implementing React add-ons and accessories.

Getting React

Now that you've read a brief overview of React, know what it is and why it matters, it is important to know the ways in which you can get React and start using it. In the React documentation, there are links to hackable JSFiddle demos where you can play around. These should be sufficient for starting to follow along with this book.

```
JSFiddle with JSX: http://jsfiddle.net/reactjs/69z2wepo/
JSFiddle without JSX: http://jsfiddle.net/reactjs/5vjqabv3/
```

Aside from in-browser development, one of the easiest ways to get React is to browse to the React getting started web site and click the big button labeled Download Starter Kit.

Download Starter Kit 0.13.1

You can of course grab the source file and add it to a script tag in your application. In fact, Facebook hosts a version of this on its CDN, links to which can be found on the React downloads page at `https://facebook.github.io/react/downloads.html`. When you have React as a script tag, the variable `React` will be a global object and you can access it once the page has loaded the React asset.

Increasingly common, you will see people who are integrating React into their workflows with Browserify or WebPack tools. Doing so allows you to `require('React')` in a way that is compatible with CommonJS module-loading systems. To get started with this process, you need to install React via npm:

```
npm install react
```

Components

Components are the core of React and the view to your application. These are typically created by utilizing a call to `React.createClass()` as follows:

```
var MyClass = React.createClass({

        render: function() {
                return (
                  <div>hello world</div>
                );
        }
});
```

or by using ES6 classes such as this one:

```
class MyClass extends React.Component {

        render() {
                return <div>hello world</div>;
        }
}
```

You will see much more about React components in the next chapter.

Virtual DOM

Perhaps the most important part of React is the concept of the *virtual DOM*. This was alluded at the beginning of this chapter, where you read about Facebook rebuilt the interface each time the data changed or the user interacted with the application. It was noted that even though Facebook realized that the performance of the fledgling framework was not performant to its standards, it still wanted to work with that ideal. So Facebook set out to change the framework from that of a set of DOM mutations each time the data changed, to what it called *reconciliation*. Facebook did this by creating a virtual DOM that they use each time they encounter an update to calculate the minimum set of changes needed to update the application's actual DOM. You learn more about this process in Chapter 2.

JSX

You learned earlier that *JSX* is the transform layer that transforms XML syntax for writing React components into the syntax that React uses to render elements in JavaScript. This is not a required element of React, but it is most definitely highly regarded and can make building applications much smoother. The syntax can accept not only custom React classes, but also plain HTML tags. It translates the tags into the appropriate React elements, as shown in the following example.

```
// JSX version

React.render(
    <div>
        <h1>Header</h1>
    </div>
);

// This would translate to

React.render(
    React.createElement('div', null,
        React.createElement('h1', null, 'Header')
    );
);
```

You will see this all in detail when you read through the JSX in-depth overview in Chapter 3.

Properties

Properties are commonly referenced in React as this.props, because that is the most frequent way that properties are accessed. *Properties* are the set of options that a component holds. this.props is a plain JavaScript object in React. These properties will not change throughout the lifecycle of the component, so you should not treat them as if they were not immutable. If you want to alter something on the component, you will be altering its state and you should utilize the state object.

State

State is set on each component as it is initialized and is also altered throughout the lifecycle of a component. The state should not be accessed from outside of the component, unless a parent component is adding or setting the initial state of the component. In general though, you should try to author your components with as little state objects as possible. This is because as you add state, the complexity of components increases because the React component will not change over time depending on the state. If it can be avoided, it is acceptable to not have any state in a component at all.

Flux

Flux is a project that is closely related to React. It's important to understand how it works with React. Flux is Facebook's application architecture for how to get data to interact with React components in an organized and meaningful way. Flux is not a Model-View-Controller architecture because those utilize a bi-directional data flow. Flux is essential to React because it helps to promote the use of React components in the way they are intended. Flux does this by creating a one-directional data flow. Data flows through three main portions of the Flux architecture: the dispatcher, the stores, and finally the React views. There is not much more to say about Flux here, but in Chapters 5 and 6 you will get a thorough introduction to Flux and then learn to integrate it into your React application to complete the introduction to React.

Tools

There are several tools that can help make React development even more fun. To access the JSX transformer that can be installed for the command-line via npm, use this command:

```
npm install -g react-tools
```

There are several utilities and editor integrations, most of which are listed at https://github.com/facebook/react/wiki/Complementary-Tools#jsx-integrations. You will likely find the tools you need there. For example, if you use *Sublime Text* or *vim* for authoring JavaScript, there is a syntax highlighter for both of these.

Another useful tool is to *lint* your code. JSX provides some special challenges for linting your files, and there is a jsxhint project, which is a JSX version of the popular JSHint linting tool.

As you are developing, you will most likely eventually need to inspect your React project in the browser. Currently there is Chrome Extension found at https://chrome.google.com/webstore/detail/react-developer-tools/fmkadmapgofadopljbjfkapdkoienihi that allows you to inspect your React components directly. You can get valuable information about props, state, and all the details you need when debugging or optimizing your React application.

Add-Ons

Facebook has provided several experimental add-ons to React on the React.addons object. These are only accessible by utilizing the /react-with-addons.js file when you are developing your application. Alternatively, if you are using Browserify or WebPack via the React npm package, you can alter your require() statement from require('react'); to require('react/addons'). You can find the documentation about which add-ons are currently available at the React site at https://facebook.github.io/react/docs/addons.html.

In addition to these add-ons, there are several community add-ons that can be very useful to React development. The number of these is growing, but one example of a useful addition is a project called *react-router*, which provides routing for React applications.

```
var App = React.createClass({
  getInitialState: function() {
  },
  render: function () {
    return (
      <div>
        <ul>
          <li><Link to="main">Demographics</Link></li>
          <li><Link to="profile">Profile</Link></li>
          <li><Link to="messages">Messages</Link></li>
        </ul>
        <UserSelect />
      </div>

      <RouteHandler name={this.state.name}/>
      </div>
    );
  }
});

var routes = (
  <Route name="main" path="/" handler={App}>
    <Route name="profile" handler={Profile}/>
    <Route name="messages" handler={Messages}/>
    <DefaultRoute handler={ Demographics }/>
  </Route>
);

Router.run(routes, function (Handler, state) {
  React.render(<Handler />, document.getElementById("content"));
});
```

This example shows how the Router handles the menu selection and will move to the appropriate component from the Router. This is a powerful extension to React. You can get by without it, but it makes things easier. The React community is large and growing fast. You will likely encounter new add-ons, or can even create your own in the process of building your great React applications. In the next chapter, you will see more of the core of React and learn how it works, which will help you further grasp what React is and why it matters.

Summary

This chapter introduced the concepts that allowed Facebook to build React. You learned how the concepts of React are commonly viewed as diverting from the normally accepted best practices in user interface development. Challenging the status quo and testing theories allowed React to become a highly performant and scalable JavaScript framework for building user interfaces.

You also saw directly, through a few examples, how React differs from some of the leading Model-View-Controller frameworks by solving the view part of these frameworks in a new way.

In the end, you were able to get a look at the terminology, concepts, and tools that make up the React framework and its community. In the next chapter, you will get a deeper look at how to use React and how it functions.

CHAPTER 2

■ ■ ■

The Core of React

In the last chapter you got a taste of what React is and why it matters to you as a developer. It showcased how React compares to other frameworks and highlighted how it is different. There were several concepts that were introduced, but not covered in the detail that an introductory book should do. This chapter will cover the building blocks of React—its core structure and architecture—in depth.

For this chapter and the others that follow, you will be presented with React code, both from the application examples and some of the inner workings of React. For the React code that composes the library, you will notice that the code is marked as such with a caption stating from where in the source it originated. The example code is written in at least one of two forms. One form (commonplace among developers today) is ECMAScript 5 syntax. Where applicable, you'll see duplicated examples using the ECMAScript 2015 (ES6) syntax, which is becoming more prevalent with React and is being incorporated as a first class citizen in the React landscape. You will find that most of the examples utilize the JSX syntax, which is covered in depth in Chapter 3.

React

As we get started looking at React, it is best to start with the React object itself. The React object contains several methods and properties that allow you to utilize react to its full potential. The chapter's source is available for most examples on jsfiddle.net or jsbin.com. The links to these examples, when available, are included in the listing captions.

React.createClass

The createClass method will create a new component class in React. createClass can be created with an object, which must have a render() function. You will get more in-depth information about components a little later in the section, but the basic implementation of createClass is as follows, where specification is the object that will contain the render() method.

```
React.createClass( specification );
```

Listing 2-1 shows how a simple component is created using createClass. This component simply creates a div element and passes a name property to that div to be rendered.

Listing 2-1. createClass. Example Available Online at
https://jsfiddle.net/cgack/gmfxh6yr/

```
var MyComponent = React.createClass({
  render: function() {
    return (
      <div>
        {this.props.name}
      </div>
    );
  }
});
```

```
React.render(<MyComponent name="frodo" />, document.getElementById('container'));
```

As you will also see when components are covered in detail later in the chapter, it is possible to create components using ES6 classes by inheriting from React.Component. This can be seen in Listing 2-2.

Listing 2-2. ES6 Class Component. Available Online at
http://jsbin.com/hezewe/2/edit?html,js,output

```
class MyComponent extends React.Component {
  render() {
    return (
      <div>
        {this.props.name}
      </div>
    );
  }
};
```

```
React.render(<MyComponent name="frodo" />, document.getElementById('container'));
```

React.Children.map

React.Children.map is a function within React.Children. It's an object that holds several helper functions that allow you to easily work with your components properties this.props.children, which will perform a function on each of the immediate children contained and will return an object. The usage for React.Children.map is as follows

```
React.Children.map( children, myFn [, context])
```

Here, the children argument is an object containing the children you want to target. The function, myFn, is then applied to each of the children. The final argument, context, is optional and will set this on the mapping function.

Listing 2-3 shows exactly how this works by creating two children elements inside of a simple component. Then, within the render method of the component, a console.log() statement is set so that you can see that the children object ReactElements are displayed.

Listing 2-3. Using React.Children.map. Available Online at https://jsfiddle.net/cgack/58u139vd/

```
var MyComponent = React.createClass({
  render: function() {
        React.Children.map(this.props.children, function(child){
          console.log(child)
      });
    return (
      <div>
        {this.props.name}
      </div>
    );
  }
});

React.render(<MyComponent name="frodo" >
    <p key="firsty">a child</p>
    <p key="2">another</p>
</MyComponent>, document.getElementById('container'));
```

React.Children.forEach

forEach is another utility that can be used on this.props.children in React. It is similar to the React.Children.map function except that it does not return an object.

```
React.Children.forEach( children, myFn [, context])
```

Listing 2-4 shows how the forEach method can be used. Similar to the map method, this example logs the ReactElement children objects to the console.

Listing 2-4. Using React.Children.forEach. Available Online at https://jsfiddle.net/cgack/vd9n6weg/

```
var MyComponent = React.createClass({
  render: function() {
        React.Children.forEach(this.props.children, function(child){
          console.log(child)
      });
```

```
    return (
      <div>
        {this.props.name}
      </div>
    );
  }
});

React.render(<MyComponent name="frodo" >
    <p key="firsty">a child</p>
    <p key="2">another</p>
</MyComponent>, document.getElementById('container'));
```

React.Children.count

The count method will return the number of components that are contained in
`this.props.children`. The function is executed as follows and accepts a single argument,
an object.

```
React.Children.count( children );
```

Listing 2-5 shows an example where `React.Children.count()` is called and the
count is logged to the console.

Listing 2-5. `React.Children.count()`. Also Available Online at
https://jsfiddle.net/cgack/n9v452qL/

```
var MyComponent = React.createClass({
  render: function() {
        var cnt = React.Children.count(this.props.children);
        console.log(cnt);
    return (
      <div>
        {this.props.name}
      </div>
    );
  }
});

React.render(<MyComponent name="frodo" >
    <p key="firsty">a child</p>
    <p key="2">another</p>
</MyComponent>, document.getElementById('container'));
```

React.Children.only

The only method will return the only child that is in this.props.children. It accepts children as a single object argument, just as the count function.

```
React.Children.only( children );
```

Listing 2-6 shows how you can utilize this method. Bear in mind that React will not allow you to call this method if your component as more than one child.

Listing 2-6. React.Children.only. Available Online at https://jsfiddle.net/cgack/xduw652e/

```
var MyComponent = React.createClass({
  render: function() {
        var only = React.Children.only(this.props.children);
        console.log(only);
    return (
      <div>
        {this.props.name}
      </div>
    );
  }
});

React.render(<MyComponent name="frodo" >
    <p key="firsty">a child</p>
</MyComponent>, document.getElementById('container'));
```

React.createElement

The createElement method will generate a new ReactElement. It is created using at least one, and optionally up to three, arguments to the function—a string type, optionally an object props, and optionally children. You will learn more about the createElement function later in the chapter.

```
React.createElement( type, [props[, [children ...] ] );
```

Listing 2-7 shows how you can create an element using this function. In this case instead of using the JSX <div> tag, you are creating an element explicitly.

Listing 2-7. createElement

```
var MyComponent = React.createClass({
  displayName: "MyComponent",

  render: function render() {
    return React.createElement(
      "div",
      null,
      this.props.name
    );
  }
});

React.render(React.createElement(MyComponent, { name: "frodo" }),
document.getElementById("container"));
```

React.cloneElement

This method will clone a ReactElement based on a target base element provided as a parameter. Optionally, you can accept a second and third argument—props and children. You will see more about the cloneElement function as we cover elements and factories in more detail later in this chapter.

```
React.cloneElement( element, [props], [children ...] );
```

React.DOM

This object provides utility functions that help to create DOM elements if you are not utilizing JSX. Instead of just writing <div>my div</div> in JSX, you could create the element by writing something like the following.

```
React.DOM.div(null, "my div");
```

Since most of the examples in this book will utilize JSX, you may not see much more of the React.DOM while writing your code. Just understand that the underlying JavaScript that the JSX transpiles to will contain these methods.

React.createFactory

React.createFactory is a function that will call createElement on a given ReactElement type. You will learn more about factories when elements and factories are covered in depth later in this chapter.

```
React.createFactory( type );
```

React.render

React.render will take a ReactElement and render it to the DOM. React only knows where to place the element by you providing it with a container, which is a DOM element. Optionally, you can provide a callback function that is executed once the ReactElement has been rendered to the DOM node.

```
React.render( element, container [, callback ] );
```

Listing 2-8 highlights the render method of a simple React component. Note that the DOM element with the ID of container is where React will render this component.

Listing 2-8. React.render. Available Online at https://jsfiddle.net/cgack/gmfxh6yr/

```
var MyComponent = React.createClass({
  render: function() {
    return (
      <div>
        {this.props.name}
      </div>
    );
  }
});

React.render(<MyComponent name="frodo" />, document.getElementById('container'));
```

React.renderToString

React.renderToString is a function that will allow you to render a ReactElement to its initial HTML markup. As you might assume, this is not as useful in the web browser as it would be on a server-side rendered version of your React application. This feature is used to serve your application from the server. In fact, if you call React.render() on an element that has been rendered with React.renderToString on the server, React is smart enough to only need to attach event handlers to that element and not remanipulate the entire DOM structure.

```
React.renderToString( reactElement );
```

React.findDOMNode

React.findDOMNode is a function that will return the DOM element of the supplied React component or element that is passed into the function:

```
React.findDOMNode( component );
```

It does this by first checking if the component or element is null. If so, it will return null. It then checks if the component passed is itself a DOM node, in which case it will return that element as the node. It will then utilize the internal ReactInstanceMap, and then fetch the DOM node from that map.

In the next sections, we will get more in-depth information concerning React components and Elements factories and discuss how they all apply to your React applications.

Discovering React Components

React components are the main building blocks when you are structuring a React application. This section you will demonstrate how components are created and what you can do with them.

React components are created when you extend from the base React.Component class using ES6. Or, more traditionally, you can use the React.createClass method (see Listings 2-9 and 2-10).

Listing 2-9. myComponent class Created Using ES6. Example Found Online at https://jsbin.com/jeguti/2/edit?html,js,output

```
class myComponent extends React.Component {
     render() {
             return ( <div>Hello World</div> );
     }
}
```

Listing 2-10. myComponent Created Using React.createClass. An interactive Version of this Example Can Be Found Online at https://jsbin.com/wicaqe/2/edit?html,js,output

```
var myComponent React.createClass({
     render: function() {
             return ( <div>Hello World</div> );
     }
});
```

React components have their own API that contains several methods and helpers, described next. Some of these functions are not available or are deprecated in React v 0.13.x as of this writing, but were present in legacy versions of the React framework. You will see these mentioned, but the focus will be on the most future friendly features, especially those accessible using ECMAScript 2015 (ES6).

The base React.Component class is the future friendly version of the component API. This means that it only implements the ES6 features, setState and forceUpdate. To use setState, you can either pass a function or a plain object to the setState method. Optionally, you can add a callback function that will be executed once the state has been set. See Listing 2-11.

Listing 2-11. setState Using a Function, the currentState Passed into the Function Will Alter the Returned (New) State Being Set

```
setState( function( currState, currProps ) {
    return { X: currState.X + "state changed" };
});
```

setState using an object directly setting the state.

```
setState( { X: "state changed" } );
```

When setState is called, you are really queuing the new object into the React update queue, which is the mechanism React uses to control when things are changed. Once the state is ready to alter, the new state object, or partial state, will be merged with the remainder of the components state. The actual update process is a handle in a batch update, so there are several caveats you should be aware of when using the setState function. First, there is no guarantee that your updates will be processed in any particular order. Because of this, if there is something that you wish to depend on once the setState has been executed, it is a good idea to do so within the callback function, which you can optionally pass to the setState function.

An important note about state is that you should never directly alter the state of a component by setting the this.state object directly. The idea here is that you want to treat the state object as immutable and only allow React and the setState process of queuing and merging state to control changes to state.

The other core API method present in the React.Component class's prototype is a function called forceUpdate. What forceUpdate does is exactly what you would expect; it forces the component to update. It does so by once again utilizing React's queue system and then forcing the component to update. It does this by bypassing one portion of a component's lifecycle, ComponentShouldUpdate, but you will learn more about the component lifecycle in a later section. In order to force an update all you need to do is call the function. You can optionally add a callback function that will execute once the update has been forced.

```
forceUpdate( callback );
```

There are several other parts to the component API that are worth mentioning because, although they are deprecated features, they are still prevalent in many implementations and much of the documentation you will see about React may include these features. Just note that these features are deprecated. In future versions of React, such as versions greater than 0.13.x, they will most likely be removed. These methods will be covered in the next section.

Understanding Component Properties and Methods

You have now seen forceUpdate and setState, the two core functions that are part of the ES6 version of React.Component class's prototype. There are several methods that are not available to you when using ES6 because they have been deprecated. Even though they not necessary when creating a component with React, you will find a lot of documentation and examples that include them, so we mention them methods here, in this introductory book.

These methods are only available when you utilize React.createClass as your function to author a component. They are added in a clever way in the React code, which I think is worth mentioning because it highlights how this is truly a bolt-on solution that will easily be dropped in future versions. The code that adds these extra functions is as follows:

```
var ReactClassComponent = function() {};
assign(
  ReactClassComponent.prototype,
  ReactComponent.prototype,
  ReactClassMixin
);
```

Here you see that the ReactClassComponent—which becomes your component when you call React.createClass—is created, and then the assign method is called. The assign method is based on Object.assign(target, ...sources) and it will take all the enumerable own properties of the sources and assign them to the target. This is basically a deep merge. In the end the ReactClassMixin is added to the component and has several methods. One method is a cousin to setState, called replaceState. The replaceState function will completely overwrite any of the states that are currently part of the component.

```
replaceState( nextState, callback );
```

The method signature includes an object that represents the nextState and an optional callback function to be executed once the state has been replaced. In general, you want your state to maintain a consistent type of signature throughout the lifecycle of your component. Because of this, replaceState should be avoided in most cases because it goes against that general idea, and state can still be manipulated utilizing setState.

Another function that is part of the ReactClassMixin, and thus available to you when creating a component using React.createClass, is the Boolean isMounted. isMounted will return true if the component that you are referencing has been rendered to the DOM.

```
bool isMounted();
```

getDOMNode is a deprecated feature that can be accessed from a component created with React.createClass. This is actually just a utility to access React.findDOMNode, which should be the preferred method for finding the DOM node where the component or element is located.

When working with React components, you may find it necessary to trigger another render of your component. The best way, which you will see, is to simply call the render() function on the component. There is another way to trigger the rendering of your component, similar to setState, and it is called setProps.

```
setProps( nextProps, callback );
```

What setProps does is allows you pass the next set of props to the component that's in the form of an object. Optionally, you can add a callback function that will execute once the component has rendered again.

Similar to the setProps method is the replaceProps function. This function accepts an object and will completely overwrite the existing set of props on the component. replaceProps also allows for an optional callback function that will execute once the component has been completely re-rendered in the DOM.

This concludes the essentials features of the React components, as well as the basic properties and functions available to you as a developer. The next section looks at the lifecycle of a component, including how it renders, before looking into React elements and factories.

Component Lifecycle and Rendering

Before you dive full ahead into the React component lifecycle, you first should learn about the component specification functions. These are the functions that will be, or can be, included in your specification object when you're creating a component. Part of these specification functions are lifecycle functions, which when encountered, will show the details as to when they execute during the life of a component.

render

As mentioned in the core API review at the beginning of this chapter, every React component must have a render function. This render function will accept a ReactElement and provide a container location where the component will be added or mounted to the DOM.

getInitialState

This function will return an object. The contents of this object will set the state of the component when it initially renders. This function is invoked one time, just before the component renders. When creating a component using ES6 classes, you will actually be setting the state, via this.state, within the constructor function of the class. Listing 2-12 shows how to handle this in both a non-ES6 component and an ES6 component.

getDefaultProps

When a ReactClass is first created, getDefaultProps is invoked one time and then is cached. This function returns an object that will represent the default state of this.props on the component. Values for this.props that do not exist in the parent component, but are present in the component's mapping, will be added to this.props here. When you're creating a component using the ES6 setting, the default props is done within the constructor function of your component class.

Listing 2-12 showcases getInitialState and getDefaultProps for both the React.createClass method of authoring components and also using ES6.

Listing 2-12. getDefaultProps and getInitialState in Action

```
var GenericComponent = React.createClass({
        getInitialState: function() {
                return { thing: this.props.thingy };
        },

        getDefaultProps: function() {
                return { thingy: "cheese" }
        }
});

// ES6

class GenericComponent extends React.Component {
        constructor(props) {
                super(props);
                this.state = { thing: props.thingy };
        }
}

GenericComponent.defaultProps = { thingy: "cheese" };
```

Mixins

A *mixin* in the component specification is an array. A mixin can share the lifecycle events of your component and you can be assured that the functionality will execute during the proper time during the component's lifecycle. An example mixin is a timer control that merges the lifecycle events of a SetIntervalMixin with the main component called TickTock. This is shown in Listing 2-13.

Listing 2-13. Using a React Mixin. An Interactive Example Is Found Online at https://jsfiddle.net/cgack/8b055pcn/

```
var SetIntervalMixin = {
  componentWillMount: function() {
    this.intervals = [];
  },
  setInterval: function() {
    this.intervals.push(setInterval.apply(null, arguments));
  },
  componentWillUnmount: function() {
    this.intervals.map(clearInterval);
  }
};
```

```
var TickTock = React.createClass({
  mixins: [SetIntervalMixin], // Use the mixin
  getInitialState: function() {
    return {seconds: 0};
  },
  componentDidMount: function() {
    this.setInterval(this.tick, 1000); // Call a method on the mixin
  },
  tick: function() {
    this.setState({seconds: this.state.seconds + 1});
  },
  render: function() {
    return (
      <p>
        React has been running for {this.state.seconds} seconds.
      </p>
    );
  }
});
```

propTypes

propTypes is an object that you can add checks for types for each of the props passed to your component. propTypes are set based on a React object called React.PropTypes, they types of which are discussed next.

If you want to enforce a specific type of prop, you can do that in several ways. First you make the property have a type, but make it an optional prop. You do this by specifying the name of the prop in your propTypes object and setting it to the corresponding React.PropTypes type. For example, a prop that is an optional Boolean would look like the following:

```
propTypes: {
    optionalBoolean: React.PropTypes.bool
}
```

The same format would work for other JavaScript types:

```
React.PropTypes.array
React.PropTypes.bool
React.PropTypes.func
React.PropTypes.number
React.PropTypes.object
React.PropTypes.string
React.PropTypes.any
```

In addition to these types, you can also make them required props by appending the isRequired tag to the React.PropType declaration. So in the case of your Boolean propType, you would now make it required as follows:

```
propTypes: {
    requiredBoolean: React.PropTypes.bool.isRequired
}
```

Outside of the JavaScript types, you may want to enforce something that is more React-specific. You can do this using the React.PropType.node, which represents anything that React can render, such as numbers, strings, elements, or an array of those types.

```
myNodeProp: React.PropTypes.node
```

Also available is the React.PropTypes.element type. It will enforce that the prop is a React element:

```
myNodeProp: React.PropTypes.element
```

There are several PropType helpers as well, shown here.

```
//enforces that your prop is an instance of a class
React.PropTypes.instanceOf( MyClass ).

// Enforces that your prop is one of an array of values
React.PropTypes.oneOf( [ 'choose', 'cheese' ])

// Enforces a prop to be any of the listed types
React.PropTypes.onOfType( [
    React.PropTypes.string,
    React.PropTypes.element,
    React.PropTypes.instanceOf( MyClass )
])

// Enforce that the prop is an array of a given type
React.PropTypes.arrayOf( React.PropTypes.string )

// Enforce the prop is an object with values of a certain type
React.PropTypes.objectOf( React.PropTypes.string )
```

statics

In your component specification, you can set an object of static functions within the statics property. Your static functions live in the component and can be invoked without creating instances of the function.

displayName

displayName is a property that is used when you see debugging messages from your React app.

componentWillMount

componentWillMount is a lifecycle event that React uses during the process of taking your component class and rendering it to your DOM. The componentWillMount method is executed once before the initial render of your component. The unique thing about componentWillMount is that if you call your setState function within this function, it will not cause a re-render of your component because the initial render method will receive the modified state.

```
componentWillMount()
```

componentDidMount

componentDidMount is a function that's invoked only on the client side of React processing, after the component has been rendered to the DOM. At this point, the React component has become a part of the DOM and you can access it using the React.findDOMNode function, you saw earlier in this chapter.

```
componentDidMount()
```

componentWillReceiveProps

As you can likely tell from the name, componentWillReceiveProps is executed when the component will be receiving props. This function is invoked every time that there is a prop change, but never on the first render. You can call setState inside this function and you will not cause an additional render. The function that you provide will have an argument for the next props object that is going to become part of the component's props. Within this function though you still have access to the current props using this.props so you can make any logic comparisons between this.props and nextProps in this function.

```
componentWillReceiveProps( nextProps )
```

shouldComponentUpdate

This function is invoked before a component renders and each time a change in prop or state is received. It will not be called before the initial render, or when forceUpdate is utilized. This function is a mechanism that you can use to skip rendering if you know that the changes to the props or state will not actually require the component to update. To short-circuit the render process, you need to return false in the function body, based on whatever criteria you determine. Doing this will bypass the rendering of the component, by not only skipping the render() function but also the next steps in the lifecycle—componentWillUpdate and componentDidUpdate

```
shouldComponentUpdate( nextProps, nextState );
```

componentWillUpdate

componentWillUpdate is invoked right before a render occurs on your component. You cannot use setState in this function.

```
componentWillUpdate( nextProps, nextState )
```

componentDidUpdate

componentDidUpdate is executed just after all the rendering updates are processed into the DOM. Since this is based on an update, it is not part of the initial render of the component. The arguments available to this function are the previous props and previous state.

```
componentDidUpdate( prevProps, prevState );
```

componentWillUnmount

As mentioned earlier, when a component is rendered to the DOM, it is called mounting. It follows then that this function, componentWillUnmount, would be invoked immediately before the component is no longer going to be mounted to the DOM.

```
componentWillUnmount()
```

Now that you have seen all the properties and lifecycle methods available to you when creating a React component, it's a good time to take a look at what the different lifecycles look like visually. Listing 2-14 shows the lifecycle of React during the initial render.

Listing 2-14. Lifecycle During Initial Render

```
var GenericComponent = React.createClass({
    // Invoked first
    getInitialProps: function() {
        return {};
    },

    // Invoked Second
    getInitialState: function() {
        return {};
    },
```

36

```
    // Third
    componentWillMount: function() {
    },

    // Render - Fourth
    render: function() {
        return ( <h1>Hello World!</h1> );
    },

    // Lastly
    componentDidMount: function() {
    }
});
```

The visual representation of Listing 2-14 is shown in Figure 2-1, where you can see the process that React components follow as they go through their initial render.

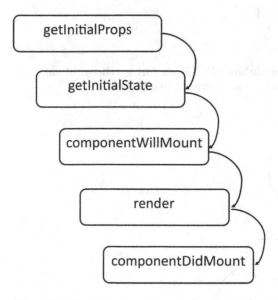

Figure 2-1. *Function invocation order during the initial render of a React component*

React also has a specific lifestyle it follows during a change of state. This is shown in Listing 2-15.

Listing 2-15. Lifecycle During Change of State

```
var GenericComponent = React.createClass({

    // First
    shouldComponentUpdate: function() {
    },

    // Next
    componentWillUpdate: function() {
    },

    // render
    render: function() {
        return ( <h1>Hello World!</h1> );
    },

    // Finally
    componentDidUpdate: function() {
    }
});
```

Just as Listing 2-15 shows you the code lifecycle of React during a change of state, Figure 2-2 visually shows the lifecycle for the same state change process.

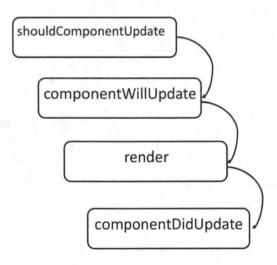

Figure 2-2. *Component lifecycle that happens when the state changes on a component*

Listing 2-16 shows a code example highlighting the lifecycle events that are processed during a React component as the props are altered.

Listing 2-16. Component Lifecycle for Props Alteration

```
var GenericComponent = React.createClass({

    // Invoked First
    componentWillReceiveProps: function( nextProps ) {
    },

    // Second
    shouldComponentUpdate: function( nextProps, nextState ) {
        // if you want to prevent the component updating
        // return false;
        return true;
    },

    // Third
    componentWillUpdate: function( nextProps, nextState ) {
    },

    // Render
    render: function() {
        return ( <h1> Hello World! </h1> );
    },

    // Finally
    componendDidUpdate: function() {
    }
});
```

The code in Listing 2-16 shows the process during a React component's props alteration. This can be visualized as shown in Figure 2-3.

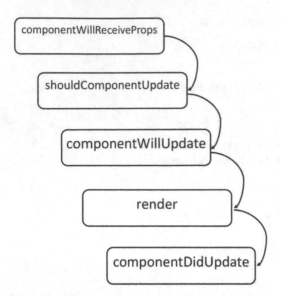

Figure 2-3. *Lifecycle of a component when it has altered props*

It is important to understand where the functions fit into the component lifecycle, but it is also important to note that render() is still the only function that's required to be part of the component specification. Let's look at one more example, using code to view a React component with all of the specification methods shown.

React Elements

You can create a React element using JSX, which you will see in detail in the next chapter, or you can create one using React.createElement. React.createElement is the same as JSX because that is what JSX uses after it is transpiled to JavaScript, as you saw at the beginning of this chapter. However, one thing to note is that the elements that are supported when using createElement are not the full set of elements supported by all web browsers. The HTML elements that are supported are shown in Listing 2-17.

Listing 2-17. HTML Elements That Are Supported When Creating a ReactElement

```
a abbr address area article aside audio b base bdi bdo big blockquote body
br button canvas caption cite code col colgroup data datalist dd del details
dfn dialog div dl dt em embed fieldset figcaption figure footer form h1 h2
h3 h4 h5 h6 head header hr html i iframe img input ins kbd keygen label
legend li link main map mark menu menuitem meta meter nav noscript object
ol optgroup option output p param picture pre progress q rp rt ruby s samp
script section select small source span strong style sub summary sup table
tbody td textarea tfoot th thead time title tr track u ul var video wbr
```

Of course, in addition to these elements you can always utilize React.createElement to create a custom of composite called ReactClass, which could fill the gap if there is a particular element that you are looking to fulfill. Other additions to these HTML elements are the supported HTML attributes, shown in Listing 2-18.

Listing 2-18. HTML Attributes Available To Be Used When Creating React Elements

```
accept acceptCharset accessKey action allowFullScreen allowTransparency alt
async autoComplete autoFocus autoPlay cellPadding cellSpacing charSet
checked classID className colSpan cols content contentEditable contextMenu
controls coords crossOrigin data dateTime defer dir disabled download
draggable encType form formAction formEncType formMethod formNoValidate
formTarget frameBorder headers height hidden high href hrefLang htmlFor
httpEquiv icon id label lang list loop low manifest marginHeight marginWidth
max maxLength media mediaGroup method min multiple muted name noValidate
open optimum pattern placeholder poster preload radioGroup readOnly rel
required role rowSpan rows sandbox scope scoped scrolling seamless selected
shape size sizes span spellCheck src srcDoc srcSet start step style tabIndex
target title type useMap value width wmode data-* aria-*
```

React Factories

React.createFactory, as you saw at the beginning of this chapter, is basically just another way that you can create React elements. As such, it is capable of rendering all of the previous sections, HTML tags, and HTML attributes along with custom ReactClass elements. A basic example of when you need a factory is when you are implementing an element without JSX.

```
// button element module
class Button {
    // class stuff
}

module.exports = Button;

// using the button element
var Button = React.createFactory(require('Button'));

class App {
  render() {
    return Button({ prop: 'foo '}); // ReactElement
  }
}
```

The main use case for factories is when you decide not to write your application using JSX like in the previous example. This is because when you create a ReactClass utilizing JSX, the transpiler process will create the requisite factories needed to properly render the element. So the JSX version, which includes the equivalent of the previous code with the factories, looks like the following.

```
var Button = require('Button');
class App {
  render() {
    return <Button prop="foo" />; // ReactElement
  }
}
```

Summary

This chapter covered the core of React. You learned about the React API, including how to create components using React.createClass. You also learned how to use the React.Component class when you are building your application using ES6 tools. Other API methods were all of the React.Children utilities, React.DOM, React.findDOMNode, and React.render.

After this initial introduction to the React core, you were introduced to the details of implementing React components, including what properties and attributes they can contain, and the various differences in lifecycle functions and the rendering processes.

Finally, you read a bit more detail regarding ReactElements and factories so that you can take the dive into understanding JSX in the following chapter. Once you read about JSX, you will be able to dive in fully to create a React application, step-by-step, and put all of this information together.

■ ■ ■

CHAPTER 3

JSX Fundamentals

In the first chapter, you read about the case for why you should use React, and the benefits that React carries with it. The second chapter showcased the important core functions of React and how you can leverage the internal API of React—ReactElements and ReactComponents—in order to understand how to build a capable React application.

In each of these chapters JSX was shown or at least mentioned. JSX is not required to work with React, but it can make authoring components much easier. JSX allows you to create JavaScript objects, which are either DOM elements or ReactComponents from an XML-like syntax. This chapter will showcase what JSX can do, and how you can utilize it in your React applications.

Why Use JSX Instead of Conventional JavaScript?

You now understand that JSX is not required to write good React code. It is, however, a commonly accepted way of writing React. The reason that this is so is precisely the reason, or reasons, why you might want to write your React code with JSX instead of plain JavaScript.

First, JSX has a familiar look and feel that developers and designers like. It is XML-like, or perhaps more appropriately HTML-like, in its structure. This means that you can approach structuring your React code in the same way that you would structure your HTML. This is not a new concept. Being able to render your application from JavaScript, while maintaining the layout and structure of an HTML-like document, is the basis of most every templating language on the web today.

Second, JSX is still JavaScript. It may not appear to be that way, but JSX is compiled through the JSX compiler, either at build time or during development in the browser, and it converts everything to maintainable React JavaScript. What JSX brings is a less verbose way of doing the same JavaScript that you would be writing anyway.

Finally, to quote the Facebook page that's drafting an official specification for JSX as an extension of ECMAScript, which defines the purpose of such specification:

> *... is to define a concise and familiar syntax for defining tree structures with attributes. A generic but well defined syntax enables a community of independent parsers and syntax highlighters to conform to a single specification.*
>
> *Embedding a new syntax in an existing language is a risky venture. Other syntax implementors or the existing language may introduce another incompatible syntax extension.*
>
> *Through a stand-alone specification, we make it easier for implementors of other syntax extensions to consider JSX when designing their own syntax. This will hopefully allow various new syntax extensions to coexist.*
>
> *It is our intention to claim minimal syntactic real estate while keeping the syntax concise and familiar. That way we leave the door open for other extensions.*
>
> *This specification does not attempt to comply with any XML or HTML specification. JSX is designed as an ECMAScript feature and the similarity to XML is only for familiarity.*

https://facebook.github.io/jsx/

It should be noted that Facebook has no intention to implement JSX within ECMAScript itself, but utilizes this document to propose JSX as an extension. But invoking the ECMAScript body then leads to the question of whether you should embrace the template literals that are already implemented into ES6. This is a valid argument, but if you examine the following examples, Listings 3-1 and 3-2, you will see the benefit of the concise JSX syntax.

Listing 3-1. Template Literals

```
var box = jsx`
  <${Box}>
    ${
      shouldShowAnswer(user) ?
      jsx`<${Answer} value=${false}>no</${Answer}>` :
      jsx`
        <${Box.Comment}>
        Text Content
        </${Box.Comment}>
        `
    }
  </${Box}>
`;
```

Listing 3-2. JSX

```
var box =
  <Box>
    {
      shouldShowAnswer(user) ?
      <Answer value={false}>no</Answer> :
      <Box.Comment>
         Text Content
      </Box.Comment>
    }
  </Box>;
```

The template literal shows that the possibility exists if Facebook had wanted to leverage this feature to build their templating into React. It does become clear, however, that this syntax is more verbose and seems noisy with extra features like the back ticks, dollar signs, and curly braces.

Compare this syntax to the JSX version. The JSX version is immediately readable and accessible to anyone familiar with XML syntax and hierarchy. Facebook argues that if they went the template literal route, then the tooling that currently exists and is being created for working with template literals would need to be updated, including the ECMAScript definition of the template literals. This is because JSX would become tightly coupled with ECMAScript standards and the processing needed to make this simple extension a part of the greater language definition, thus JSX is its own entity.

You see the benefits that JSX brings. It is more concise to write, yet it still lends itself to transpiling into robust JavaScript that is necessary to power your React applications. It is also, in general, more approachable to anyone who is familiar with HTML syntax. This is not only your leading JavaScript developers, but also the designers— if you split roles in such a way—of your project can have access to structuring the output of your React components with JSX.

Using a JSX Transformer

In the previous chapter, you learned briefly how to get React up and running in a browser or text editor. This section will provide more details about how you can go about setting up a development environment that can leverage the power of the JSX transformer.

It is possible to simply go to the React web site at https://facebook.github.io/react/docs/getting-started.html and go to their "React JSFiddle" link. This will allow you to utilize React in the browser, with JSX. This is a great way to follow along with the examples in this book if you do not want to set up a fully-fledged development environment.

Another way is to integrate React and the JSX transformer script into an HTML file that you are utilizing to develop your React application. One way to do this is to download React and the JSX transformer from the React web site, or to link from the Facebook CDN.

This approach is perfect for development, but because of the extra script and processing that happens on the client when you include this, it is recommended that you precompile your JSX before moving to production.

```
<script src="https://fb.me/react-0.13.2.js"></script>
<script src="https://fb.me/JSXTransformer-0.13.2.js"></script>
```

There are of course other ways to get an environment set up. You need Node.js and npm installed on your machine.

First, to get the JSX tooling you simply need to install the react-tools package from npm.

```
npm install -g react-tools
```

You can then watch any directory filled with *.jsx files and output them to a compiled JavaScript directory, like the following. This will look at the src directory and output to the build directory.

```
jsx --watch src/ build/
```

Another way, which will also allow for easy transpiling of ES6 modules and components, is to leverage several npm packages and a Node.js utility to watch for changes and transpile on the fly.

In order to get started with this setup, you need to install a few global tools via npm. First is *browserify*, which is a tool allowing you to use the CommonJS require("module") syntax within a browser environment, outside of Node.js. In addition to browserify, you can utilize *watchify* to watch a directory or file and transform it with a module called *babel*. Babel is a module that will convert anything you have written using ES6 and make it compatible with ECMAScript version 5 (ES5) syntax. Babel will also convert JSX to the appropriate JavaScript. The commands needed to do this are outlined in the following code.

```
# first you need to globally acquire browserify, watchify, and babel
npm install -g browserify watchify babel

# next in the directory in which you wish to develop your application

npm install react browserify watchify babelify --save-dev
```

You now have the toolchain which will allow you to create your .jsx files and render them as complete JavaScript and React components in the browser. To do this, you can create a src and a dist directory, where the src directory will hold your JSX file. For this example, assume there is a single file called app.jsx. This will then compile to a bundle.js file that resides in the dist folder. To direct watchify and babelify to transform the JSX file into bundle.js the command should be as follows.

```
watchify -t babelify ./src/app.jsx -o ./dist/bundle.js -v
```

Here you invoke watchify, which will watch for a file and transform (-t) the file using babel (babelify) transformations. The next argument is the source file to transform followed by the output (-o) file and the destination directory and file (bundle.js). The –v flag signifies verbose, so each time the input file (app.jsx) is changed, you will see the output of the transform in your console. This will look something like the following:

```
624227 bytes written to ./dist/bundle.js (0.29 seconds)
624227 bytes written to ./dist/bundle.js (0.18 seconds)
624183 bytes written to ./dist/bundle.js (0.32 seconds)
```

You can then create an HTML file that contains a reference to bundle.js, which will have the JavaScript for React and the transformed JSX.

```
<!DOCTYPE html>
<html lang="en">
<head>
        <meta charset="UTF-8">
        <title>Introduction to React<title>
</head>
<body>
        <div id="container"></div>
        <script src="dist/bundle.js"></script>
</body>
</html>
```

■ **Note**   Using babelify to convert your JSX to JavaScript is not the only method. In fact there are many other solutions you can utilize, including, but not limited to, gulp-jsx (https://github.com/alexmingoia/gulp-jsx) and reactify (https://github.com/andreypopp/reactify). You should be able to find a tool that fits your workflow if the method outlined in this section does not.

How JSX Converts from an XML-Like Syntax to Valid JavaScript

The most basic explanation for how JSX is capable of taking XML-like syntax and converting it into the JavaScript that's utilized to generate React elements and components is that it simply scans the XML-like structure and replaces the tags with the functions needed in the JavaScript.

You will see several examples of how you can take a snippet of JSX and convert it into the proper JavaScript to be used with your React application. Listing 3-3 shows a simple "Hello World" application.

47

Listing 3-3. Original JSX Version of a Simple Hello World Application

```
var Hello = React.createClass({
    render: function() {
        return <div>Hello {this.props.name}</div>;
    }
});

React.render(<Hello name="World" />, document.getElementById('container'));
```

You can see in this example that the JSX creates a div element that also holds a reference to the this.props.name property. This is all contained within a component called Hello. Later on in the application you call React.render() on the Hello component, passing a value of "World" to the name property, which will become this.props.name. Listing 3-4 shows what this transforms into, after the React JSX transformer does the work to turn this XML-like syntax into JavaScript.

Listing 3-4. Post-JSX Transformation of the Hello World Example

```
var Hello = React.createClass({displayName: "Hello",
    render: function() {
        return React.createElement("div", null, "Hello ", this.props.name);
    }
});

React.render(React.createElement(Hello, {name: "World"}),
document.getElementById('container'));
```

First, notice that in this simple example, these two examples are not dissimilar to a manner where one might be favored over the other. There is just a little bit more verbosity in the way in which the post-JSX transformed source reads. A few things to point out are that there is an automatically injected displayName. This happens only if you have not already set this property on your ReactComponent specification when creating your React component. It does this by checking each of the properties on the component object and checking if the value of displayName exists. If not, it will append the displayName to the component, as you see in the example.

Another item of note for this component is the actual structure of how the JSX syntax is broken down into a ReactElement. This is where the JSX transformer takes the XML-like structure

```
<div>Hello {this.props.name}</div>
```

And turns it into a JavaScript function:

```
React.createElement("div", null, "Hello ", this.props.name);
```

In the previous chapter, the details of React.createElement showed that it accepts at least one argument, a type, and several optional arguments. In this case, the type is a div, with a null object specifying any attributes on the object. Then the children's "Hello" text will become the innerHTML of the div element. The props, specifically this.props.name, are also passed. This is all handled in the JSX transformer code where the objective is to build a string that represents the functioning JavaScript for an element. The source of this is interesting to read, so you can get a glimpse of what the transform is doing if you care to read through the transformer source code.

The main idea of the transform is to account for everything and smartly compile the string that will represent the JavaScript version of a JSX component. Another portion of this example that was transformed was the final render, which went from this:

```
<Hello name="World" />
```

To this:

```
React.createElement(Hello, {name: "World"})
```

This might seem to you like the same transform that happened with your div element, but the difference is that in this case there is a non-null property object representing the name property. This is where the this.props.name from the Hello component comes from. It is a direct attribute on the element when React.render() is called. You see that there is a logical process where these JSX elements are parsed and then are subsequently rebuilt into valid JavaScript, which React can utilize to mount components to the page. This is just a trivial example. Next you will see what happens when you start to nest JSX elements within each other.

To showcase how nested custom ReactComponents are transformed from JSX to JavaScript, you will now see a convoluted example of the same "Hello World" greeting in Listing 3-5.

Listing 3-5. Hello World Greeting

```
var GreetingComponent = React.createClass({
    render: function() {
        return <div>Hello {this.props.name}</div>;
        }
});

var GenericComponent = React.createClass({
    render: function() {
        return <GreetingComponent name={this.props.name} />;
    }
});

React.render(<GenericComponent name="World" />,
document.getElementById('container'));
```

49

Here you see a GenericComponent, which is just a container div that holds another componented GreetingComponent. The GenericComponent is rendered by calling an attribute, similar to how Hello component in the previous example. However, here there is a secondary layer of ReactComponent that passes the this.props.name as an attribute to its child element. Naturally, you would not want to make an interface that looks like this in the real world, but you would not be in the business of making Hello components either. You can assume that this is just an example to showcase how JSX transpiles nested components. The result of the JSX transformation is shown in Listing 3-6.

Listing 3-6. JSX Transform of GenericComponent

```
var GreetingComponent = React.createClass({displayName: "GreetingComponent",
    render: function() {
        return React.createElement("div", null, "Hello ", this.props.name);
    }
});

var GenericComponent = React.createClass({displayName: "GenericComponent",
    render: function() {
        return React.createElement(GreetingComponent, {name:
        this.props.name});
    }
});

React.render(React.createElement(GenericComponent, {name: "World"}),
document.getElementById('container'));
```

At first glance this is not very different from the conversion of the trivial Hello World example, but upon closer examination, you will see that there is more at work here to help you understand JSX better. For this example, you can start by examining the React.render() function call, which converts the following:

```
<GenericComponent name="World" />
```

into this:

```
React.createElement(GenericComponent, {name: "World"})
```

This is exactly what happens when you created your Hello component in the Hello World example, where the name attribute is converted into a property to be passed to the GenericComponent. Where this diverges is in the next level, where the GenericComponent is created and references the GreetingComponent, thereby passing the name attribute directly to the GreetingComponent.

```
<GreetingComponent name={this.props.name} />
```

This shows how you can process an attribute and pass it to the child elements. Starting from a top-level attribute on the GenericComponent, you can pass this attribute by using this.props to the child element GreetingComponent. It's also important to see that the GreetingComponent is created, just like any other ReactComponent or HTML tag, and there is nothing inherently special about nesting components versus nesting HTML tags in your React component structure.

One thing to note about ReactComponents versus a plain HTML tag is that React utilizes, by convention, uppercase letters to begin names for components and lowercase for HTML tags.

There are times when you need a more cleverly designed interface, and even the simplest forms are built in a structured way. In JSX you can do this by creating each component, and then building the hierarchy according to a nesting of variables that are added to the scope, such as when you're creating a form with nested labels and inputs. While this method works well, it does have some limitations and is perhaps not necessary when creating separate component variable names for items that belong to the same grouping. In this case, a form is built as a part of the parent FormComponent. The good news is that React knows this is unnecessary and allows you to author components that are namespaced to a parent. In Listing 3-7, you will see the creation of a FormComponent namespace with multiple related components that will be nested within it. This is then rendered utilizing a component alias and then the components are namespaced for the render.

Listing 3-7. Creating FormComponent

```
var React = require("react");

var FormComponent = React.createClass({
        render: function() {
                return <form>{this.props.children}</form>;
        }
});

FormComponent.Row = React.createClass({
        render: function() {
                return <fieldset>{this.props.children}</fieldset>;
        }
});

FormComponent.Label = React.createClass({
        render: function() {
                return <label htmlFor={this.props.for}>{this.props.text}
                {this.props.children}</label>;
        }
});
```

```
FormComponent.Input = React.createClass({
        render: function() {
                return <input type={this.props.type} id={this.props.id} />;
        }
});

var Form = FormComponent;
var App = (
        <Form>
                <Form.Row>
                        <Form.Label text="label" for="txt">
                                <Form.Input id="txt" type="text" />
                        </Form.Label>
                </Form.Row>
                <Form.Row>
                        <Form.Label text="label" for="chx">
                                <Form.Input id="chx" type="checkbox" />
                        </Form.Label>
                </Form.Row>
        </Form>
);

React.render(App, document.getElementById("container"));
```

Once the JSX has been transformed into the JavaScript, you get the example shown in Listing 3-8.

Listing 3-8. JSX Transformed for the FormComponent

```
var React = require("react");

var FormComponent = React.createClass({
        displayName: "FormComponent",

        render: function render() {
                return React.createElement(
                        "form",
                        null,
                        this.props.children
                );
        }
});

FormComponent.Row = React.createClass({
        displayName: "Row",
```

```
        render: function render() {
                return React.createElement(
                        "fieldset",
                        null,
                        this.props.children
                );
        }
});

FormComponent.Label = React.createClass({
        displayName: "Label",

        render: function render() {
                return React.createElement(
                        "label",
                        { htmlFor: this.props["for"] },
                        this.props.text,
                        this.props.children
                );
        }
});

FormComponent.Input = React.createClass({
        displayName: "Input",

        render: function render() {
                return React.createElement("input", { type: this.props.type,
                id: this.props.id });
        }
});

var Form = FormComponent;
var App = React.createElement(
        Form,
        null,
        React.createElement(
                Form.Row,
                null,
                React.createElement(
                        Form.Label,
                        { text: "label", "for": "txt" },
                        React.createElement(Form.Input, { id: "txt",
                        type: "text" })
                )
        ),
        React.createElement(
                Form.Row,
                null,
```

```
        React.createElement(
                Form.Label,
                { text: "label", "for": "chx" },
                React.createElement(Form.Input, { id: "chx",
                type: "checkbox" })
            )
        )
);
```

```
React.render(App, document.getElementById("container"));
```

From this example there is a great deal to learn, not just about nesting and namespacing, but also about how React can pass the children element in this.props.children. It is important to note that when you are working with nested elements that you hold a reference to them within the JSX of your previous element. If you were to create a FormComponent element that looked like the following, it would never hold a nested child.

```
var FormComponent = React.createComponent({
    render: function() {
        return <form></form>;
    }
});
```

In this example, even if you had set up the render to look like the following example, it would still return just the form because there is no reference to the children of the element.

```
<FormComponent>
    <FormRow />
</FormComponent>
```

As you saw in the correct example, there is a simple way to get these elements to nest properly using this.props.children:

```
var FormComponent = React.createClass({
        render: function() {
                return <form>{this.props.children}</form>;
        }
});
```

Once you get to the point where you have the ability to pass children, you can structure your React application components like Listing 3-9 shows. All of the nesting will then work as you expect.

Listing 3-9. Passing Children

```
var App = (
        <Form>
                <Form.Row>
                        <Form.Label text="label" for="txt">
                                <Form.Input id="txt" type="text" />
                        </Form.Label>
                </Form.Row>
                <Form.Row>
                        <Form.Label text="label" for="chx">
                                <Form.Input id="chx" type="checkbox" />
                        </Form.Label>
                </Form.Row>
        </Form>
);
```

Spread Attributes and Other Considerations for JSX

By now, you have likely come to realize that JSX is essentially a custom templating engine for React and for writing React components. It makes it easier to author and structure your application and allows the code for your user interfaces to be more accessible to all the members of your team. This section outlines some of the templating considerations as well as some other special characteristics involved when using JSX with React.

Spread attributes are a concept derived from ES6 arrays and from early work on the ES7 specification. They play an interesting role with your JSX code for React because they allow you to add properties that you may not have known about when you originally authored the component. For this example, imagine that your trivial Hello World application, which accepts the parameter name, now needs a custom message after the greeting. In this case, you could add another named parameter, message, which would then be used just as the name property was, or you could utilize spread attributes and create a greeting object that holds both name and message. What this looks like in practice is shown in Listing 3-10.

Listing 3-10. Using Spread Attributes

```
var greeting = {
        name: "World",
        message: "all your base are belong to us"
};

var Hello = React.createClass({
    render: function() {
        return <div>Hello {this.props.name}, {this.props.greeting}</div>;
    }
});

React.render(<Hello {...greeting} />, document.getElementById("container"));
```

You can see that instead of the named properties on the component in the render function, you now utilize three dots and the name of an object, which represents the spread attributes. Then each of the properties attached to this object are accessible in the component. The this.props.name and this.props.greeting are being utilized in the component JSX.

Another version of this same application is shown in Listing 3-11. This time note that it is authored in ES6 and that the JavaScript output from a JSX component is slightly different. It's more verbose than components authored using React.createClass.

Listing 3-11. Spread Attributes with ES6

```
var greeting = {}
greeting.name = "World";
greeting.message = "All your base are belong to us.";

class Hello extends React.Component {
    render() {
        return (
                <div>Hello {this.props.name}, {this.props.message}</div>
        );
    }
}

React.render(<Hello {...greeting} />, document.getElementById("container"));
```

You can see that there isn't much difference in the way you create a simple component here with JSX. Listing 3-12 shows that the actual result of the JSX transform from the ES6 module looks slightly different.

Listing 3-12. Transform of the Component

```
 var greeting = {};
greeting.name = "World";
greeting.message = "All your base are belong to us.";

var Hello = (function (_React$Component) {
        function Hello() {
                _classCallCheck(this, Hello);

                if (_React$Component != null) {
                        _React$Component.apply(this, arguments);
                }
        }

        _inherits(Hello, _React$Component);
```

```
    _createClass(Hello, [{
        key: "render",
        value: function render() {
            return React.createElement(
                "div",
                null,
                "Hello ",
                this.props.name,
                ", ",
                this.props.message
            );
        }
    }]);

    return Hello;
})(React.Component);

React.render(React.createElement(Hello, greeting),
document.getElementById("container"));
```

The impressive thing you might notice about the way that the spread attributes are rendered is that there is no extra functionality built into the transformed component that indicates that the props came from a spread attribute.

The benefits here might not be substantial to everyone who uses React, but you can see that this could make for a much more concise way of adding multiple properties to components instead of specifying each one as its own attribute in the JSX.

If you look at the earlier form example where each of the HTML for, id's, and input types were all explicitly declared. By utilizing the spread attributes, you could see that if the input data were coming from an API or JSON object, it could easily be composed into the component. This is shown in Listing 3-13.

Listing 3-13. Input Types and Spread Attributes

```
var input1 = {
    "type": "text",
    "text": "label",
    "id": "txt"
};

var input2 = {
    "type": "checkbox",
    "text": "label",
    "id": "chx"
};
```

```
var Form = FormComponent;
var App = (
        <Form>
                <Form.Row>
                        <Form.Label {...input1} >
                                <Form.Input {...input1} />
                        </Form.Label>
                </Form.Row>
                <Form.Row>
                        <Form.Label {...input2}>
                                <Form.Input {...input2} />
                        </Form.Label>
                </Form.Row>
        </Form>
);
```

One particular use case you might encounter when building a React application using JSX is if you're wanting to add some logic to your components. This would be something like an if-else or for loop within your JSX.

When rendering items such as for loops, you need only to remember that you can write JavaScript in your component's render function. The simple loop example shown in Listing 3-14 iterates over an array and adds list items to an unordered list. It's quite easy to render once you realize that you do not need to learn any tricks.

Listing 3-14. Looping in JSX

```
class ListItem extends React.Component {
        render() {
                return <li>{this.props.text}</li>;
        }
}

class BigList extends React.Component {
        render() {
                var items = [ "item1", "item2", "item3", "item4" ];
                var formattedItems = [];
                for (var i = 0, ii = items.length; i < ii; i++ ) {
                        var textObj = { text: items[i] };
                        formattedItems.push(<ListItem {...textObj} />);
                }
                return <ul>{formattedItems}</ul>;
        }
}

React.render(<BigList />, document.getElementById("container"));
```

This JSX takes the array of formatted items, which calls the ListItem component, and passes the spread attribute object to that component. Those are then added to an unordered list that's returned via the render function. The transformed JSX looks just as you would expect, including the for loop as it was authored. It's shown in Listing 3-15.

Listing 3-15. Transformed JSX for BigList

```
var ListItem = (function (_React$Component) {
        function ListItem() {
                _classCallCheck(this, ListItem);

                if (_React$Component != null) {
                        _React$Component.apply(this, arguments);
                }
        }

        _inherits(ListItem, _React$Component);

        _createClass(ListItem, [{
                key: "render",
                value: function render() {
                        return React.createElement(
                                "li",
                                null,
                                this.props.text
                        );
                }
        }]);

        return ListItem;
})(React.Component);

var BigList = (function (_React$Component2) {
        function BigList() {
                _classCallCheck(this, BigList);

                if (_React$Component2 != null) {
                        _React$Component2.apply(this, arguments);
                }
        }

        _inherits(BigList, _React$Component2);

        _createClass(BigList, [{
                key: "render",
                value: function render() {
                        var items = ["item1", "item2", "item3", "item4"];
                        var formattedItems = [];
```

```
                        for (var i = 0, ii = items.length; i < ii; i++) {
                                var textObj = { text: items[i] };
                                formattedItems.push(React.
                                createElement(ListItem, textObj));
                        }
                        return React.createElement(
                                "ul",
                                null,
                                formattedItems
                        );
                }
        }]);

        return BigList;
})(React.Component);

React.render(React.createElement(BigList, null),
document.getElementById("container"));
```

Another common task when utilizing a templating language is the if-else
statement. In React, there are a couple of ways this sort of conditional can happen.
First, as you might assume, you can handle your if conditional within the logic of your
application within the JavaScript of the component, just as you saw with the previous for
loop. This would look something like Listing 3-16, whereby if users are not signed in, they
will get a "Sign In" button; otherwise, they get the user's menu.

Listing 3-16. Using Conditionals in JSX

```
var SignIn = React.createClass({
        render: function() {
                return <a href="/signin">Sign In</a>;
        }
});

var UserMenu = React.createClass({
        render: function() {
                return <ul className="usermenu"><li>Item</li><li>
                Another</li></ul>;
        }
});

var userIsSignedIn = false;
var MainApp = React.createClass({
        render: function() {
                var navElement;
```

60

```
                 if (userIsSignedIn) {
                         navElement = <UserMenu />;
                 } else {
                         navElement = <SignIn />;
                 }

                 return <div>{navElement}</div>;
        }
});

React.render(<MainApp />, document.getElementById("container"));
```

This example, once transformed into the appropriate JavaScript, would appear as shown in Listing 3-17.

Listing 3-17. Transformed Conditional

```
var SignIn = React.createClass({
        displayName: "SignIn",

        render: function render() {
                return React.createElement(
                        "a",
                        { href: "/signin" },
                        "Sign In"
                );
        }
});

var UserMenu = React.createClass({
        displayName: "UserMenu",

        render: function render() {
                return React.createElement(
                        "ul",
                        { className: "usermenu" },
                        React.createElement(
                                "li",
                                null,
                                "Item"
                        ),
                        React.createElement(
                                "li",
                                null,
                                "Another"
                        )
                );
        }
});
```

61

```
var userIsSignedIn = false;
var MainApp = React.createClass({
        displayName: "MainApp",

        render: function render() {
                var navElement;
                if (userIsSignedIn) {
                        navElement = React.createElement(UserMenu, null);
                } else {
                        navElement = React.createElement(SignIn, null);
                }

                return React.createElement(
                        "div",
                        null,
                        navElement
                );
        }
});

React.render(React.createElement(MainApp, null),
document.getElementById("container"));
```

So in summary here, you can use JavaScript to manipulate your components. However, if you want to embed the logic more tightly within your components, you can do that as well by using ternary operators in your code, as shown in Listing 3-18.

Listing 3-18. Ternary Operators in JSX

```
var SignIn = React.createClass({
        render: function() {
                return <a href="/signin">Sign In</a>;
        }
});

var UserMenu = React.createClass({
        render: function() {
                return <ul className="usermenu"><li>Item</li><li>Another
                </li></ul>;
        }
});
```

```
var userIsSignedIn = true;
var MainApp = React.createClass({
    render: function() {
        return <div>{ userIsSignedIn ? <UserMenu /> :
        <SignIn /> }</div>;
    }
});
```

```
React.render(<MainApp />, document.getElementById("container"));
```

The JavaScript after the JSX transformation is shown in Listing 3-19.

Listing 3-19. Ternaries Transformed

```
var SignIn = React.createClass({
    displayName: "SignIn",

    render: function render() {
        return React.createElement(
            "a",
            { href: "/signin" },
            "Sign In"
        );
    }
});

var UserMenu = React.createClass({
    displayName: "UserMenu",

    render: function render() {
        return React.createElement(
            "ul",
            { className: "usermenu" },
            React.createElement(
                "li",
                null,
                "Item"
            ),
            React.createElement(
                "li",
                null,
                "Another"
            )
        );
    }
});
```

63

```
var userIsSignedIn = true;
var MainApp = React.createClass({
        displayName: "MainApp",

        render: function render() {
                return React.createElement(
                        "div",
                        null,
                        userIsSignedIn ? React.createElement(UserMenu, null)
                        : React.createElement(SignIn, null)
                );
        }
});

React.render(React.createElement(MainApp, null),
document.getElementById("container"));
```

Summary

In this chapter, you saw JSX in action. You learned how JSX transforms from the XML-like syntax that many are familiar with to the JavaScript necessary for React to utilize it when creating components and building your application.

You also saw how you can incorporate JSX into your workflow when building an application, or when utilizing many of the tools to incorporate JSX while you are just developing and learning React.

Finally, you saw not only how it works, but several examples of how you can utilize JSX to build logical templates and nested elements within your React application. All of this will help you understand what happens in the next chapter, when you will walk through the creation of a full React application from wireframing to the final product.

■ ■ ■

CHAPTER 4

Building a React Web Application

In the previous three chapters you were given an arsenal of information about React. Starting with what React is and how it differs from other JavaScript and user interface frameworks, you received a firm foundation for understanding the way React works. From there you were introduced to the core concepts of React and the features that come with it. Things like component creation and the rendering lifecycle were introduced. In the last chapter you were introduced to a powerful tenant in the React world, JSX. With JSX, you saw how you can succinctly create React components in an approachable and perhaps more maintainable way, compared to a plain JavaScript implementation.

This chapter will showcase how you can build a React application by taking into consideration a non-React application and breaking it down into the components you need. You will then be able to split that into the React application and you will see the value that React can bring even to an application that isn't at the scale of Facebook or Instagram.

Outlining Your Application's Basic Functionality

There are several ways that you can outline your application's basic functionality that will be transferred into a React application. One way is to wireframe a design. This is especially helpful if you don't have an active web application, but instead are considering creating the application structure from a blank slate, powered with React. This wireframing process is obviously important for any application, but can substantially aide in the process of identifying where you should split your application into different components.

Before you get started wireframing, you need an idea for an application. I created a workout diary/log where I can store various workouts and view my history of efforts. This sort of project is a great example of how different frameworks work together and integrate into a workflow. Your example application might be different, but for the purposes of this book, you will follow along with the workout application motif. What follows is the thought process involved in brainstorming and wireframing your application.

So now you have an idea for your application. You need to identify the main areas of functionality that will represent the entire picture of this application. For this workout application, you need a way for the users to authenticate to the application because each user will want to record her or his own workout data. Once the users are authenticated, there should also be a page or form where users can define and categorize the workouts they will be logging. This would be something that allows a defined name and a type, such as "For Time," "Max Weight," "Number of Repetitions". These different types will come into play in the next section, which allows the users to store their workouts. When they are storing a workout and the Type is time-related, you may choose to have a specific form field that indicates a way to log the time taken to complete the work. Similar specific fields for Max Weight and Number Of Repetitions would be available as well, but only shown for specific work types. This specificity of types allows users to categorize their workouts differently in the History section of the application. Perhaps they can even plot over time the different efforts for each workout.

Now what you have is a basic, prose version, outline of the application's functionality. You are probably seeing this in a React mindset by now, but you need to take it to the next step of seeing this application as a wireframe.

Thinking in Terms of Components

Building on the outline created in the previous section, you will now encounter two scenarios for how to build you application. One way, as mentioned previously, is to create wireframes that follow the outline of your application. This gives you a fresh start to identify where you can create components that fit into your new React application. The other method is to base the structure on an existing application and its source in order to break down the functionality into components. You will first look at a set of wireframes for your application, and then you will see an example of an existing application that will need to be rewritten as a React application.

Wireframes

When creating wireframes you can choose to use the back of a napkin, MS Paint, or any number of tools that help you express your ideas in images that describe the experience. What follows are the sections of the application that I decided to break apart into React components. At the root of all of the components is the app, and it will be a parent component to all of the following nested components. If you choose not to use wireframes and instead prefer to dissect your application using existing code, you can just skim this subsection and pick up at "Rewriting an Existing Application" to discover the insights to thinking in terms of components.

The Sign In screen shown in Figure 4-1 is of a simple authentication component. This is actually an entire component. In reality, you might choose to make this component one of a two-part authentication component.

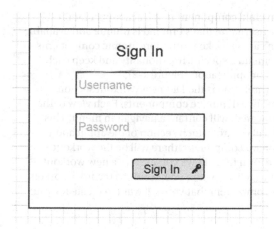

Figure 4-1. *Sign In component wireframe*

This Sign In component might not require any child components because you likely will be posting this form to your authentication server to validate. The other React component that might make up this authentication section is a Create An Account screen.

In a Create An Account component, shown in Figure 4-2, you can see there is again a simple form just like the Sign In form. The difference here is that you need a password-validation component. This would ensure any password rules you have are enforced and would also check against the second password field to ensure that the values match. In your application you might also choose to include a reCAPTCHA or some other component that would make sure that whomever is creating an account is not a robot.

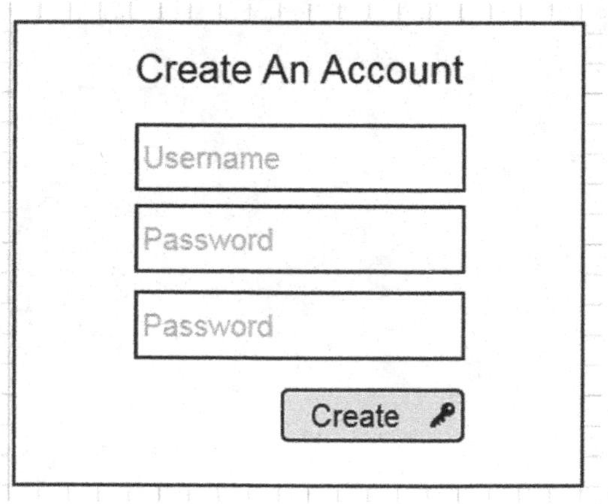

Figure 4-2. *Account creation component wireframe*

Along with the password-validation child component in the account creation component, you need to ensure that the username that's entered is unique and available in your system. So even this simple form can be broken into more atomic components using React. This would allow you to maintain a specific functionality and keep each action separate from the other parts of your application (Figure 4-2).

The next section of the application wireframe is the Define a Workout section (Figure 4-3). This can be split into at least two definitive components. Each view of the application, once you have been authenticated, will contain a navigation menu. This menu will be a component in itself and will control which section of the application is rendered. Along with the navigation menu component, there will be the workout definition component. This will hold the form that allows you to store a new workout definition, which you will be able to return to later when you decide to record a workout you have performed. This form is also a component that you will want to create for your React application.

Figure 4-3. *Define a Workout component wireframe*

After the Define a Workout section, the next section (called Record a Workout) retains the same navigation component that you saw in the previous section (Figure 4-4). Along with the navigation component is the form that controls which workout you want to record, and the effort you will be recording. This could be a singular component, but you might find that creating a drop-down menu of available workouts is better.

Figure 4-4. Store workout component wireframe

The final section of the application is the Workout History section (Figure 4-5). This section retains the navigation component and shows a table, or a listview if you choose, of all your workouts. This table is a component in itself, so bear in mind that in a future version you may want to extend this component with a child component. This child component may search or sort the history, so it should have the props available to handle that functionality.

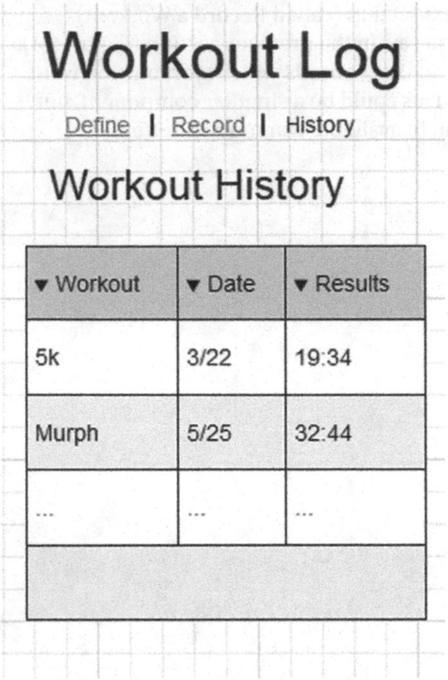

Workout Log

Define | Record | History

Workout History

▼ Workout	▼ Date	▼ Results
5k	3/22	19:34
Murph	5/25	32:44
...	...	...

Figure 4-5. *Workout History component wireframe*

Rewrite an Existing Application

In this section, you will see an existing application that you can rewrite using React. Again, the first step is to identify where you can create components, or child components within the application, just as you saw with the wireframes example.

The first portion is the authentication component, comprised of the Sign In child component and the Create An Account component. If you explore the example showing a basic HTML and jQuery application in Listing 4-1, you should be able to identify where you can create components.

Listing 4-1. Basic Markup for Authentication in Your Existing Application

```
<div id="signInForm" class="notSignedIn">
            <label for="username">Username:</label>
            <input type="text" id="username">
            <label for="password">Password:</label>
            <input type="text" id="password">
            <button id="signIn">Sign In</button>
    </div>
```

```
<div id="createAccount" class="notSignedIn">
    <label for="username">Username:</label>
    <input type="text" id="username">
    <label for="password">Password:</label>
    <input type="text" id="password">
    <label for="password">Confirm Password:</label>
    <input type="text" id="confpassword">
    <button id="signIn">Create Account</button>
</div>
```

Authentication Mechanism Using jQuery

```
$("#signIn").on("click", function() {
    // do authentication
    $(".notSignedIn").hide();
    $(".signedIn").show();
});
```

You see that there are clearly two sections for this. Perhaps you can imagine creating a component that looks like the following.

```
<Authentication>
        <SignIn />
        <CreateAccount />
</Authentication>
```

This is precisely the component that will be created in the next section. Of course, there is the functionality of actually performing the authentication, which will have to account for, but in a basic sense this is what the component will look like.

The next section is the navigation menu, which will be shared throughout the application once authentication is completed.

```
<ul id="navMenu">
    <li><a href="#defineWorkouts">Define Workouts</a></li>
    <li><a href="#logWorkout">Log Workout</a></li>
    <li><a href="#viewHistory">View History</a></li>
    <li><a href="#logout" id="logout">Logout</a></li>
</ul>
```

This navigation menu will be rewritten in JSX so that it can be easily reused in each component that will require it. The next sections of the jQuery/HTML version of the application are basic submitable areas that take the value from the specific fields and submit them upon clicking. For example, the Define Workout section looks like Listing 4-2.

Listing 4-2. Save a Workout Definition in HTML/jQuery

```
<div id="defineWorkouts" class="tabview">
    <label for="defineName">Define Name</label>
    <input type="text" id="defineName">
    <label for="defineType">Define Type</label>
    <input id="defineType" type="text">
    <label for="defineDesc">Description</label>
    <textarea id="defineDesc" ></textarea>
    <button id="saveDefinition">Save Definition</button>
</div>
```

The other two sections, Record a Workout and Workout History, follow the same form with the exception that there is a portion of the component that comes from the stored workouts (Listings 4-3 and 4-4).

Listing 4-3. The Record a Workout Section—Different Workouts Are Available from Defined Workouts in #chooseWorkout and Pulled from a Data Store

```
<div id="logWorkout" class="tabview">
        <label for="chooseWorkout">Workout:</label>
        <select name="" id="chooseWorkout">
                <!-- populated via script -->
        </select>
        <label for="workoutResult">Result:</label>
        <!-- input based on the type of the workout chosen -->
        <input id="workoutResult" type="text" />
        <input id="workoutDate" type="date" />
        <label for="notes">Notes:</label>
        <textarea id="notes"></textarea>
</div>
```

Listing 4-4. Workout History Based on All the Work Recorded and Pulled from a Data Store

```
<div id="viewHistory" class="tabview">
        <!-- dynamically populated -->
        <ul id="history">
        </ul>
</div>
```

Now you can see that you have each of these atomic, or subatomic, snippets of code that represents a singular code path to producing a user interface component. This is exactly what you want in order to split these sections of functionality into their own components. This example was a simple workout log application. Try to examine your own source and prepare for a rewrite by cataloging which components you need to create.

Creating the Necessary Components for Your App

In the previous sections, you examined a wireframe and an existing application in order to determine which features of your application you want to split into React components, or you at least visualized where it would make sense to do so. In this section, you take the next step and start to isolate each of those components using React code in order to start building your application.

To start with, you will create the authorization component. This component, as outlined from the wireframes or the code example, consists of two child components—SignIn and CreateAccount. This entire application could live in a single file if you choose, but for maintainability it is prudent to separate components into their own files and utilize a tool like browserify or webpack in order to modularize these files. First is the signin.jsx file, followed by createaccount.jsx (Listings 4-5 and 4-6).

Listing 4-5. The signin.jsx File

```
var React = require("react");

var SignIn = React.createClass({
    render: function() {
        return (
            <div>
                <label htmlFor="username">Username
                <input type="text" id="username" />
                </label>
                <label htmlFor="password">Password
                <input type="text" id="password" />
                </label>
                <button id="signIn" onClick={this.props.onAuthComplete.bind
                (null, this._doAuth)}>Sign In</button>
            </div>
        );
    },

    _doAuth: function() {
        return true;
    }
});

module.exports = SignIn;
```

Listing 4-6. The createaccount.jsx File

```
var React = require("react");

var CreateAccount = React.createClass({
        render: function() {
                return (
                        <div>
                        <label htmlFor="username">Username:
                                <input type="text" id="username" />
                        </label>
                        <label htmlFor="password">Password:
                                <input type="text" id="password" />
                        </label>
                        <label htmlFor="password">Confirm Password:
                                <input type="text" id="confpassword" />
                        </label>
                        <button id="signIn" onClick={this.props
                        .onAuthComplete.bind( null, this._
                        createAccount)}>Create Account</button>
                        </div>
                );
        },

        _createAccount: function() {
                // do creation logic here
                return true;
        }
});

module.exports = CreateAccount;
```

Both of these components are straightforward to the point that the JSX markup looks similar to what was created in the jQuery and HTML application in the previous section. What is different is that you no longer see the binding to the button using jQuery. In its place, there is an onClick binding that then calls a reference to this.props.onAuthComplete. This might seem curious, but once you see the parent app component, it will indicate how the authorization state is handled through each child component. Listing 4-7 provides a simple component—Authentication—that contains both child authentication components. These child components are available because within the files that they were defined, we exported the component objects by leveraging module.exports. module.exports is a CommonJS mechanism that allows you to export an object that you define. Once that object is loaded using require() in a subsequent module, you can gain access to it.

Listing 4-7. The auth.jsx File

```
var React = require("react");
var SignIn = require("./signin.jsx");
var CreateAccount = require("./createaccount.jsx");

var Authentication = React.createClass({
        render: function() {
                return (
                        <div>
                                <SignIn onAuthComplete={this.props.
                                onAuthComplete}/>
                                <CreateAccount onAuthComplete={this.props.
                                onAuthComplete}/>
                        </div>
                );
        }
})

module.exports = Authentication;
```

Now you have the authentication, which is comprised of the two child components—SignIn and CreateAccount. From here you need the next major section of the application, which is everything that happens after you authenticate your application. Again this process will be split into the appropriate components, each of which is contained in its own module (Listing 4-8).

Listing 4-8. The navigation.jsx File

```
var React = require("react");

var Navigation = React.createClass({
    render: function() {
        return (
                <ul>
                        <li><a href="#" onClick={this.props.onNav.bind(null,
                        this._nav("define"))}>Define A Workout</a></li>
                        <li><a href="#"onClick={this.props.onNav.bind(null,
                        this._nav("store"))}>Record A Workout</a></li>
                        <li><a href="#"onClick={this.props.onNav.bind(null,
                        this._nav("history"))}>View History</a></li>
                    <li><a href="#" onClick={this.props.onLogout}>Logout
                        </a></li>
                </ul>
            );
        },
```

```
        _nav: function( view ) {
                return view;
        }
});
```

```
module.exports = Navigation;
```

Listing 4-8 shows the Navigation component. You will notice that there is a binding to the onClick event for each of the navigation elements. For Logout, this is a simple call to the logout mechanism that's passed to this Navigation component as a property. For the other navigation pieces, this example shows how you can locally set a value and pass it to a parent component. This is done by setting a value in the _nav function. You will see that referenced in the parent component once we have written it. Now you need to create the modules and components for defining, storing, and viewing your workout history. These are shown in Listings 4-9 through 4-11.

Listing 4-9. The define.jsx File

```
var React = require("react");

var DefineWorkout = React.createClass({
        render: function() {
                return  (
                <div id="defineWorkouts" >
                        <h2>Define Workout</h2>
                        <label htmlFor="defineName">Define Name
                                <input type="text" id="defineName" />
                        </label>
                        <label htmlFor="defineType">Define Type
                                <input id="defineType" type="text" />
                        </label>
                        <label htmlFor="defineDesc">Description</label>
                        <textarea id="defineDesc" ></textarea>
                        <button id="saveDefinition">Save Definition</button>
                </div>
                );
        }
});
```

```
module.exports = DefineWorkout;
```

The DefineWorkout component is just simple inputs and a Save Definition button. If you are hooking this application into a data store via an API, you would want to add an onClick function to the Save Definition button in order to store the data in the appropriate location.

Listing 4-10. The store.jsx File

```
var React = require("react");

var Option = React.createClass({
        render: function() {
                return <option>{this.props.value}</option>;
        }
});
var StoreWorkout = React.createClass({
        _mockWorkouts: [
                {
                        "name": "Murph",
                        "type": "fortime",
                        "description": "Run 1 Mile \n 100 pull-ups \n 200
                        push-ups \n 300 squats \n Run 1 Mile"
                },
                {
                        "name": "Tabata Something Else",
                        "type": "reps",
                        "description": "4 x 20 seconds on 10 seconds off for
                        4 minutes \n pull-ups, push-ups, sit-ups, squats"
                }
        ],

        render: function() {

                var opts = [];
                for (var i = 0; i < this._mockWorkouts.length; i++ ) {
                        opts.push(<Option value={this._mockWorkouts[i]
                        .name} />);
                }
                return (

                        <div id="logWorkout" class="tabview">
                                <h2>Record Workout</h2>
                        <label htmlFor="chooseWorkout">Workout:</label>
                        <select name="" id="chooseWorkout">
                                {opts}
                        </select>
                        <label htmlFor="workoutResult">Result:</label>
                <input id="workoutResult" type="text" />
```

77

```
                    <input id="workoutDate" type="date" />
                        <label htmlFor="notes">Notes:</label>
                        <textarea id="notes"></textarea>
                        <button>Store</button>
                </div>
                );
        }
});

module.exports = StoreWorkout;
```

StoreWorkout is a component that again holds simple form inputs to help you log your workout. The interesting part of this is the mock data of existing workouts that dynamically populate the <select/> tag. That tag holds the workouts you defined in the DefineWorkout component.

Listing 4-11. The history.jsx File

```
var React = require("react");

var ListItem = React.createClass({
        render: function() {
                return <li>{this.props.name} - {this.props.result}</li>;
        }
});

var History = React.createClass({
        _mockHistory: [
                {
                        "name": "Murph",
                        "result": "32:18",
                        "notes": "painful, but fun"
                },
                {
                        "name": "Tabata Something Else",
                        "type": "reps",
                        "result": "421",
                        "notes": ""
                }
        ],

        render: function() {
                var hist = this._mockHistory;
                var formatedLi = [];
                for (var i = 0; i < hist.length; i++) {
                        var histObj = { name: hist[i].name, result:
                        hist[i].result };
                        formatedLi.push(<ListItem {...histObj} />);
                }
```

```
        return (
                <div>
                        <h2>History</h2>
                        <ul>
                                {formatedLi}
                        </ul>
                </div>
        );
    }
});

module.exports = History;
```

History also takes mock data and adds it to the presentation layer of the application in the form of the formattedLi array of <ListItem /> components. Before you put all of these components together and run them, let's pause for a section to ponder what testing React applications entails.

Testing Your Application

React makes it easy to integrate testing frameworks into your application. This is because of the React add-on called testUtils at React.addons.testUtils. The test utilities that are available in this add-on are outlined in this section. To utilize the add-ons, you must require React add-ons by making a call such as require("react/addons") or by getting the React with add-ons source from the Facebook CDN at <script src="https://fb.me/react-with-addons-0.13.3.js"></script>.

Simulate

Simulate is a method that will utilize a simulated event so that you are capable of mocking an interaction within your React application. The method signature for utilizing Simulate is as follows:

```
React.addons.TestUtils.Simulate.{eventName}(DOMElement, eventData)
```

DOMElement is an element and eventData is an object. An example would look like this:

```
var node = React.findDOMNode(this.refs.input);
React.addons.TestUtils.Simulate.click(node);
```

renderIntoDocument

renderIntoDocument takes a component and renders it into a detached DOM node in the document. Since the method renders into a DOM, a DOM is required for this method. Therefore, if you are testing outside of a DOM, you will not be able to utilize this method.

mockComponent

This method allows you to create a fake React component. This will become a simple
`<div>` within the application unless you utilize the optional `mockTagName` parameter to
this object. This is particularly useful when you want to create a component and add
useful methods to it in your test scenario.

isElement

This function simply returns a Boolean that indicates whether the React element that is
targeted is indeed an element:

```
isElement(ReactElement element)
```

isElementOfType

This method accepts a React element and a component class function and will return
`True` if the element that you provided is of the type of the `componentClass`.

```
isElementOfType( element, componentClass)
```

isDOMComponent

This method returns the Boolean determined whether the instance of a React component
is a DOM element such as a `<div>` or `<h1>`.

isCompositeComponent

This is another Boolean check that will return `True` if the React component that's provided
is a composite component, meaning that it was created using `React.createClass` or in
ES6 extending `ReactComponent`.

isCompositeComponentWithType

Similar to `isCompositeComponent`, this method will check the `ReactComponent` instance
and compare it to the `componentClass` that is provided to the method. If the instance and
the class type provided match, this will return `True`.

findAllInRenderedTree

This method returns an array of components that exist within the tree or base component
provided that the function provided to this method tests as `True`.

```
findAllInRenderedTree( tree, test )
```

scryRenderedDOMComponentsWithClass

This method looks for DOM components in the rendered tree, such as <span> with a matching className.

```
scryRenderedDOMComponentsWithClass( tree, className)
```

findRenderedDOMComponentsWithClass

This method is the same as scryRenderedDOMComponentsWithClass, with the only difference being that the expected result is a singular component instead of an array. This means that there will be an error if more than one component is returned.

scryRenderedDOMComponentsWithTag

Returns an array starting from a tree component and matches all instances that share the same tagName.

```
scryRenderedDOMComponentsWithTag( tree, tagName)
```

findRenderedDOMComponentsWithTag

This is the same as the previous method, with the exception that it anticipates that there be a single result instead of an array. This method will create an error if more than one result is returned.

scryRenderedComponentsWithType

Similar to the previous examples but instead compares based on the componentClass, which is a function provided to this method.

```
scryRenderedComponentsWithType( tree, componentClass )
```

findRenderedComponentsWithType

Same as the previous method, once again anticipating a singular result with an error thrown if more than one result is found.

You can take all of these methods and utilize them to augment your testing tool of choice. For Facebook, that tool is Jest. In order to set up Jest on your machine, simply use npm as follows:

```
npm install jest-cli –save-dev
```

Once it's installed, you can update your application's package.json and name the test framework.

```
{
    ...
    "scripts": {
        "test": "jest"
    }
    ...
}
```

Now each time you run npm test, tests that reside in the __tests__ folder will be executed. Tests can be structured in a way that requires a module and then you can run tests on said module. A test for the SignIn component might look like the following:

```
jest.dontMock("../src/signin.jsx");

describe("SignIn", function() {
        it("will contain a Sign In button to submit", function() {
                var React = require("react/addons");
                var SignIn = require("../src/signin.jsx");
                var TestUtils = React.addons.TestUtils;

                var signin = TestUtils.renderIntoDocument(
                        <SignIn />;
                );

                var username = TestUtils.findRenderedDOMComponentWithTag(
                signin, "button" );

                expect( username.getDOMNode().textContent).equalTo("Sign In");

        });
});
```

You can see that you can leverage the TestUtils included with React add-ons to build tests that will allow you to assert the tests while building your application's test suite.

Running Your Application

In this section, you will piece together the components you have constructed into a working application. You will now take each of the components and assemble them. In this case, you will be using browserify to combine your scripts, which were modularized using CommonJS modules. You could of course combine these into a single file, or you could write them in ES6 modules similar to Listing 4-12.

Listing 4-12. signin.jsx as an ES6 Module

```
var React = require("react");

class SignIn extends React.Component {
        constructor(props) {
                super(props);
        }
        render() {
                return (
                        <div>
                        <label htmlFor="username">Username
                                <input type="text" id="username" />
                        </label>
                        <label htmlFor="password">Password
                                <input type="text" id="password" />
                        </label>
                        <button id="signIn" onClick={this.props.
                        onAuthComplete.bind( null,
                        this._doAuth)}>Sign In</button>
                        </div>
                );
        }

        _doAuth() {
                return true;
        }

}

module.exports = SignIn;
```

So, you can author your application in ES6 as well, but for this example the application will be assembled using the existing source that was written using React.createClass();.

The first thing that needs to happen is there needs to be a core app.jsx file that will contain the code and become the main entry point to the application. This file should include the necessary components to build the application. In this case, you need the main application, which you will build in a second, and the authentication module.

```
var React = require("react");
var Authentication = require("./auth.jsx");
var WorkoutLog = require("./workoutlog.jsx");

var App = React.createClass({
        getInitialState: function() {
                return { signedIn: false }
        },
```

```
    render: function() {
        return (
                <div>{ this.state.signedIn ? <WorkoutLog
                onLogout={this._onLogout} /> : <Authentication
                onAuthComplete={this._onAuthComplete}/> }</div>
        );
    },

    _onAuthComplete: function( result ) {
        // let the child auth components control behavior here
        if (result()) {
                this.setState( { signedIn: true } );
        }
    },

    _onLogout: function() {
            this.setState( { signedIn: false } )
    }
})
React.render(<App/>, document.getElementById("container"));
```

This is a single component that implements the Authentication and WorkoutLog components. There is a single-state parameter that indicates whether the user is signed in or not. This is passed from the child components by passing the props, as you saw earlier. The SignIn component binds to the click of the button, which will then essentially share the result of that click with the _onAuthComplete function. This is the same as _onLogout, which is handled in the navigation menu in the WorkoutLog component.

Speaking of the WorkoutLog component—now is the time to see it, as it is composed of all of the remaining components (Listing 4-13).

Listing 4-13. The workoutlog.jsx File

```
var React = require("react");
var Nav = require("./navigation.jsx");
var DefineWorkout = require("./define.jsx");
var StoreWorkout = require("./store.jsx");
var History = require("./history.jsx");

var WorkoutLog = React.createClass({
    getInitialState: function() {
            return { view: "define" };
    },
```

```
        render: function() {
            return (
                <div>
                    <h1>Workout Log</h1>
                    <Nav onLogout={this.props.onLogout}
                    onNav={this._onNav}/>
                    {this.state.view === "define" ?
                    <DefineWorkout /> : "" }
                    {this.state.view === "store" ?
                    <StoreWorkout /> : "" }
                    {this.state.view === "history" ?
                    <History /> : "" }
                </div>
            );
        },

    _onNav: function( theView ) {
            this.setState( { view: theView });
    }
});

module.exports = WorkoutLog;
```

WorkoutLog is a component that contains the Nav, which is then passed the prop onLogout to control the state of the <App> component. The <DefineWorkout />, <StoreWorkout />, and <History /> components are all available, but the visibility within the render mechanism is controlled by state.view, which is the only state parameter that is maintained at the WorkoutLog component level. This state is set when a link in the <Nav/> components is clicked. As long as all your paths are correct and you are using a command like this one:

```
$ watchify -t babelify ./src/app.jsx -o ./dist/bundle.js -v
```

The result will be bundled into bundle.js. You will be able to navigate to your index.html (or whatever you named your HTML document) and view your working React application. Congratulations!

Summary

In this chapter, you examined the process from conceptualization to final representation of a React web application. This included utilizing wireframing ideas to visualize where the components of your application would be split apart, or alternatively dissecting an existing application in order to prepare for a React rewrite.

You then saw how to actually create these components in a way that utilized CommonJS modules in order to keep the components isolated and maintainable. Finally, you put all of these together in a working application.

In the next chapters, you will encounter some complementary tools that will help you go even farther with your React development. For now, you have already successfully built a React application and are likely enjoying the newfound view of the web development world that React has unveiled.

CHAPTER 5

■ ■ ■

Introducing Flux: An Application Architecture for React

The first four chapters of this book introduced React, which is the JavaScript framework for creating user interfaces, a product of Facebook's engineering team. What you have seen up to this point is sufficient to create robust user interfaces using React and to implement React into your new or existing application frameworks. However, there is more than just React to the React ecosystem. One of these items is Flux, an application framework created by Facebook to complement React in a way that displaces the standard Model-View-Controller (MVC) framework. This is not because there is necessarily anything wrong with MVC as it stands, but more because when you start building an application with React and dissecting your application logic into components, you will find that a framework, similar to the typical MVC, will not be as efficient or maintainable as something like Flux, which has been designed with React in mind and also has the ability to scale your application without an increasing maintenance cost.

This chapter will outline what Flux is and how to get started with Flux, and also explores how Flux and React fit together. You will become familiar with the Flux concepts before structuring an application with Flux in the following chapter.

What Flux Is and Why It Is Different than Typical MVC Frameworks

Flux is purpose-built for React. It is an application architecture meant to eschew the concept of multi-directional data flow and binding, which is common in typical MVC frameworks. It instead offers a unidirectional data flow where React is the user interface layer in the middle. To get a better example, let's examine the typical MVC framework and look at the problems that arise when attempting to scale an application beyond its designed capacity.

In Figure 5-1, you see that there is direction that starts from an action and passes through the controller to the model.

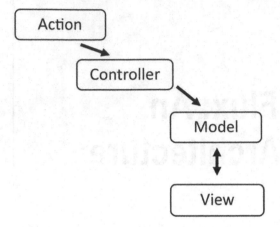

Figure 5-1. *Typical Model-View-Controller data flow model*

The Model and View can swap data back and forth. This is relatively straight-forward, but what happens if you add a few extra models and views? Then it becomes a little more complex but still something you can handle, as outlined in Figure 5-2.

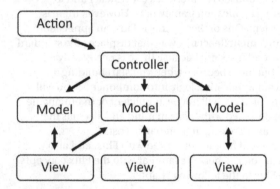

Figure 5-2. *Additional models and views added to the MVC data model*

This is clearly more complex because there are multiple views and models, some of which even share data between one another. However, this structure doesn't get completely unwieldy until there are so many models and views that you can no longer track the dependencies even in a simple model diagram, let alone figure out how the models and views interact with one another within the code itself.

What you see when it starts to become unwieldy is the same scenario that leads us to move toward React in the first place. The nesting and coupling of these dependencies causes you to have ample opportunities in which to lose track of a particular variable or relationship. This means that updating a single model or view could have detrimental effects to an unknown related view. This is not fun or maintainable. It can add hours to your development time or cause serious bugs in the form of bad user experience or even infinite update loops. This is where Flux is beneficial, especially when you have more than a few models and views.

Flux, at the most basic level, looks like Figure 5-3, with an action, dispatch, store, and view layer.

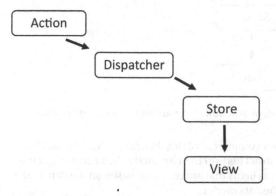

Figure 5-3. Basic Flux data flow

This is the basic structure of how data flows through a Flux application. The initial state of the data flow comes from an action. This action is then transferred to the dispatcher.

The dispatcher in a Flux application is like a traffic officer. This dispatcher will ensure that the data flowing through the application will not cause any of the cascading effects that you might see with a many model and view MVC setup. The dispatcher must also make sure that the actions are executed in the order in which they arrive so that race conditions are prevented.

The dispatcher the store takes over for each action. Once an action makes it to a store, actions are not allowed to enter into the store until the store has completed the processing of the current action. The views then respond to the store once the store has indicated that something in the data has changed.

The views themselves can contribute to this data flow by instantiating another action, which then passes through the dispatcher to the store and back to the view, as shown in Figure 5-4.

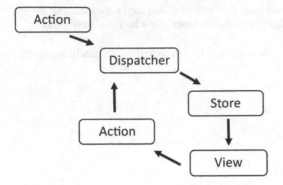

Figure 5-4. *Flux with a view creating its own action and passing that to the dispatcher*

You are likely wondering if the view component of this data flow is where React fits into Flux. Well, this is precisely where React fits into the Flux model. You can think of the React components in your application as items that are rendered based on the data that is transferred from the store portion of the data model.

What about the actions that are created from the views themselves? How does React create an action to be sent to the dispatcher? This could simply be the result of a user interaction. For example, if I have a chat application and want to filter a friend list or something similar, React will create new actions as I interact with that portion of the component and those actions will pass to the dispatcher to initiate another Flux process, as shown in Figure 5-5.

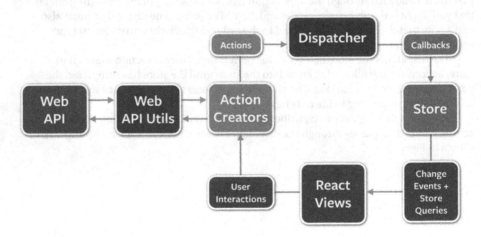

Figure 5-5. *Full Flux architecture, including calls from data stores*

Figure 5-5 shows the full lifecycle of a Flux architecture. This starts with some sort of data API, which then sends information or data to the action creators. The action creators, as the name suggests, create actions to pass to the dispatcher. The dispatcher then polices these actions and filters them to the store. The store processes the actions and pushes them to the view layer, which in this case is a collection of React components. These React components can then have user interactions that pass their events or activity to the action creators in order to continue the process. Next, you will see a more detailed breakdown of these Flux components.

The Basic Components of Flux

Flux is composed of four major components, or what can be considered at the very least to be core concepts. These are the *dispatcher, stores, actions,* and *views*, as you learned in the previous section. They are described in more detail in the following sections.

Dispatcher

The dispatcher is the epicenter of the data flow in your Flux applications. What this means is that it controls what flows into the stores of the Flux application. It does this because the stores create callbacks that are linked to the dispatcher, so the dispatcher serves as a housing place for those callbacks. Each store in the application creates a callback that registers it with the dispatcher. When an action creator sends a new action to the dispatcher, the dispatcher will ensure that all registered stores get that action because of the callback provided.

The ability for the dispatcher to actually dispatch the actions to the stores via callback is essential for larger-scale applications because the callbacks can be managed to the point where they execute in a specific order. Also, stores can explicitly wait for other stores to finish updating before they update themselves.

Stores

Stores contain the logic and state of a Flux application. You might think of these as essentially the Model portion of a traditional MVC application. The difference is that instead of representing a single data structure like a traditional model, the store in Flux can actually represent the state management of many objects. These objects represent a particular domain subset within your Flux application.

A store will register itself with a dispatcher and provide it with the callback, as was mentioned in the previous section. The callback that's passed in will have a parameter that is the action, passed to it via the dispatcher. The callback will also contain a `switch` statement that is based on the type of action and allows for the proper delegation into the function, or methods, contained internally within the store. This is what allows the store to update state via the action provided by the dispatcher. The store must then broadcast an event dictating that the state has changed so that the views can fetch the new state and update the rendering of the application.

Actions

Actions are actually any form of data that has been dispatched to the stores. You will see later in this chapter a basic example of actions and action creators for a simple TODO application using the Flux architecture.

Views

The view layer is where React fits into this architecture. React, with its ability to render the virtual DOM and minimize complex DOM updates, is particularly useful when creating a Flux application. React is not just the view in itself. In fact, React at the highest level of the view hierarchy can become a sort of controller-view, which can control the user interface and render any particular subset of your application.

When a view or controller-view receives an event from the store layer, it will first make sure that it holds the freshest data by accessing the store's getter methods. It will then use setState() or forceUpdate() in order to render() properly into the DOM. Once this happens, a controller-view's render will then propagate to all the children that it governs.

A common paradigm for passing the state of an application to a controller-view and subsequently to its child views is to pass the entire state as a single object. This provides you two benefits. First, you can see the state that will reach all parts of the view hierarchy, thus allowing you to manage it as a whole, and second, it will reduce the amount of props that you need to pass and maintain, essentially making your application much easier to maintain.

How React and Flux Look Together

Now that you have a basic understanding of how Flux and React work together and how they are utilized, the remainder of this chapter will focus on a simple TODO application. Just as the introduction to React in the earlier chapters focused on TodoMVC.com, this chapter will examine the basic TodoMVC application utilizing Flux, before moving on to a more complex chat application in the following chapter.

The HTML is similar to what you have previously seen, where you will be building all of your JavaScript resources into a single bundle.js file. To follow along, you can clone the Flux repository at https://github.com/facebook/flux.git and navigate to the examples/flux-todomvc directory. You can then use the npm install and npm start commands and navigate your browser to the index.html file to view the example. What these commands do is utilize npm to install the dependencies for the Flux examples. This includes the actual Flux npm package, which, while not a framework, includes the dispatcher and other modules that allow the Flux architecture to work properly.

■ **Note**   The code shown in Listings 5-1 through 5-10 is licensed by Facebook under a BSD License.

Listing 5-1. Index.html for TodoMVC with Flux

```
<!doctype html>
<html lang="en">
  <head>
    <meta charset="utf-8">
    <title>Flux • TodoMVC</title>
    <link rel="stylesheet" href="todomvc-common/base.css">
    <link rel="stylesheet" href="css/app.css">
  </head>
  <body>
    <section id="todoapp"></section>
    <footer id="info">
      <p>Double-click to edit a todo</p>
      <p>Created by <a href="http://facebook.com/bill.fisher.771">Bill
      Fisher</a></p>
      <p>Part of <a href="http://todomvc.com">TodoMVC</a></p>
    </footer>
    <script src="js/bundle.js"></script>
  </body>
</html>
```

The main bootstrap file that the bundle.js file is based on is the app.js file shown in Listing 5-2. This file requires React and includes a reference to the TodoApp.react module, which is the main component for the TODO application.

Listing 5-2. Main Entry app.js for the TodoMVC Flux Application

```
var React = require('react');

var TodoApp = require('./components/TodoApp.react');

React.render(
  <TodoApp />,
  document.getElementById('todoapp')
);
```

The TodoApp.react.js module, as shown in Listing 5-3, requires the Footer, Header, and MainSection components of this Flux module. In addition, you see the introduction of the stores/TodoStore module.

Listing 5-3. Todoapp.js: A Controller-View for the TodoMVC Flux Application

```
var Footer = require('./Footer.react');
var Header = require('./Header.react');
var MainSection = require('./MainSection.react');
var React = require('react');
var TodoStore = require('../stores/TodoStore');
```

```javascript
/**
 * Retrieve the current TODO data from the TodoStore
 */
function getTodoState() {
  return {
    allTodos: TodoStore.getAll(),
    areAllComplete: TodoStore.areAllComplete()
  };
}

var TodoApp = React.createClass({

  getInitialState: function() {
    return getTodoState();
  },

  componentDidMount: function() {
    TodoStore.addChangeListener(this._onChange);
  },

  componentWillUnmount: function() {
    TodoStore.removeChangeListener(this._onChange);
  },

  /**
   * @return {object}
   */
  render: function() {
      return (
    <div>
      <Header />
      <MainSection
        allTodos={this.state.allTodos}
        areAllComplete={this.state.areAllComplete}
      />
      <Footer allTodos={this.state.allTodos} />
    </div>
      );;
  },

  /**
   * Event handler for 'change' events coming from the TodoStore
   */
  _onChange: function() {
    this.setState(getTodoState());
  }

});;

module.exports = TodoApp;
```

The MainSection component follows in Listing 5-4, and is just as the title suggests—the component that controls the main portion of the TODO application. Note that it includes the first reference to the TodoActions module as well, which you will see later in this example. Aside from that, this is a React component that you would expect to see; it renders the main section, handles some React props, and inserts the TodoItems, just like the non-Flux—based React TodoMVC application you saw in the earlier chapters.

Listing 5-4. The MainSection.js Module

```
var React = require('react');
var ReactPropTypes = React.PropTypes;
var TodoActions = require('../actions/TodoActions');
var TodoItem = require('./TodoItem.react');

var MainSection = React.createClass({

  propTypes: {
    allTodos: ReactPropTypes.object.isRequired,
    areAllComplete: ReactPropTypes.bool.isRequired
  },

  /**
   * @return {object}
   */
  render: function() {
    // This section should be hidden by default
    // and shown when there are TODOs.
    if (Object.keys(this.props.allTodos).length < 1) {
      return null;
    }

    var allTodos = this.props.allTodos;
    var todos = [];

    for (var key in allTodos) {
      todos.push(<TodoItem key={key} todo={allTodos[key]} />);
    }

    return (
      <section id="main">
        <input
          id="toggle-all"
          type="checkbox"
          onChange={this._onToggleCompleteAll}
          checked={this.props.areAllComplete ? 'checked' : ''}
        />
```

95

```
      <label htmlFor="toggle-all">Mark all as complete</label>
      <ul id="todo-list">{todos}</ul>
    </section>
  );
},

/**
 * Event handler to mark all TODOs as complete
 */
_onToggleCompleteAll: function() {
  TodoActions.toggleCompleteAll();
}

});

module.exports = MainSection;
```

The TodoItems component (Listing 5-5) is very similar to the non-Flux version of this application. Note that the events bound to the DOM, just as in the MainSection, are now linked to a TodoActions function (this is shown in bold text in the examples). This allows the actions to be tied to the Flux data flow and to propagate appropriately from the dispatcher, to the store, and then finally to the view. Similar bindings to TodoActions are found in the Header (Listing 5-7) and Footer (Listing 5-6) components as well.

Listing 5-5. TodoItem.react.js

```
var React = require('react');
var ReactPropTypes = React.PropTypes;
var TodoActions = require('../actions/TodoActions');
var TodoTextInput = require('./TodoTextInput.react');

var cx = require('react/lib/cx');

var TodoItem = React.createClass({

  propTypes: {
    todo: ReactPropTypes.object.isRequired
  },

  getInitialState: function() {
    return {
      isEditing: false
    };
  },

  /**
   * @return {object}
   */
```

```
render: function() {
  var todo = this.props.todo;

  var input;
  if (this.state.isEditing) {
    input =
      <TodoTextInput
        className="edit"
        onSave={this._onSave}
        value={todo.text}
      />;
  }

  // List items should get the class 'editing' when editing
  // and 'completed' when marked as completed.
  // Note that 'completed' is a classification while 'complete' is a state.
  // This differentiation between classification and state becomes important
  // in the naming of view actions toggleComplete() vs. destroyCompleted().
  return (
    <li
      className={cx({
        'completed': todo.complete,
        'editing': this.state.isEditing
      })}
      key={todo.id}>
      <div className="view">
        <input
          className="toggle"
          type="checkbox"
          checked={todo.complete}
          onChange={this._onToggleComplete}
        />
        <label onDoubleClick={this._onDoubleClick}>
          {todo.text}
        </label>
        <button className="destroy" onClick={this._onDestroyClick} />
      </div>
      {input}
    </li>
  );
},

_onToggleComplete: function() {
  TodoActions.toggleComplete(this.props.todo);
},
```

```javascript
  _onDoubleClick: function() {
    this.setState({isEditing: true});
  },

  /**
   * Event handler called within TodoTextInput.
   * Defining this here allows TodoTextInput to be used in multiple places
   * in different ways.
   * @param  {string} text
   */
  _onSave: function(text) {
    TodoActions.updateText(this.props.todo.id, text);
    this.setState({isEditing: false});
  },

  _onDestroyClick: function() {
    TodoActions.destroy(this.props.todo.id);
  }

});

module.exports = TodoItem;
```

Listing 5-6. footer.react.js

```javascript
var React = require('react');
var ReactPropTypes = React.PropTypes;
var TodoActions = require('../actions/TodoActions');

var Footer = React.createClass({

  propTypes: {
    allTodos: ReactPropTypes.object.isRequired
  },

  /**
   * @return {object}
   */
  render: function() {
    var allTodos = this.props.allTodos;
    var total = Object.keys(allTodos).length;

    if (total === 0) {
      return null;
    }
```

```
    var completed = 0;
    for (var key in allTodos) {
      if (allTodos[key].complete) {
        completed++;
      }
    }

    var itemsLeft = total - completed;
    var itemsLeftPhrase = itemsLeft === 1 ? ' item ' : ' items ';
    itemsLeftPhrase += 'left';

    // Undefined and thus not rendered if no completed items are left.
    var clearCompletedButton;
    if (completed) {
      clearCompletedButton =
        <button
          id="clear-completed"
          onClick={this._onClearCompletedClick}>
          Clear completed ({completed})
        </button>;
    }

      return (
    <footer id="footer">
      <span id="todo-count">
        <strong>
            {itemsLeft}
        </strong>
        {itemsLeftPhrase}
      </span>
      {clearCompletedButton}
    </footer>
  );
},

/**
 * Event handler to delete all completed TODOs
 */
_onClearCompletedClick: function() {
  TodoActions.destroyCompleted();
}

});

module.exports = Footer;
```

Listing 5-7. header.react.js

```
var React = require('react');
var TodoActions = require('../actions/TodoActions');
var TodoTextInput = require('./TodoTextInput.react');

var Header = React.createClass({

  /**
   * @return {object}
   */
  render: function() {
    return (
      <header id="header">
        <h1>todos</h1>
        <TodoTextInput
          id="new-todo"
          placeholder="What needs to be done?"
          onSave={this._onSave}
        />
      </header>
    );
  },

  /**
   * Event handler called within TodoTextInput.
   * Defining this here allows TodoTextInput to be used in multiple places
   * in different ways.
   * @param {string} text
   */
  _onSave: function(text) {
    if (text.trim()){
      TodoActions.create(text);
    }

  }

});

module.exports = Header;
```

Now that you have seen how the React components send events or actions to the TodoActions module, you can examine what the TodoActions module looks like in this example. It is simply an object with methods that tie to the AppDispatcher (Listing 5-8).

Listing 5-8. appdispatcher.js

```
var Dispatcher = require('flux').Dispatcher;

module.exports = new Dispatcher();
```

The AppDispatcher is a simple instance of the base Flux dispatcher, as you see in the previous example. You see that the TodoActions functions, shown in Listing 5-9, each have something to do with the AppDispatcher. They call the dispatch function, which holds an object that describes what is being dispatched from the dispatcher AppDispatcher.dispatch(/* object describing dispatch */); You can see that the object that's dispatched varies based on which action is called. This means that the create function will produce a dispatch with an object that contains the TodoConstants. TODO_CREATE actionType passing the text of the TodoItem.

Listing 5-9. Todoactions.js

```
var AppDispatcher = require('../dispatcher/AppDispatcher');
var TodoConstants = require('../constants/TodoConstants');

var TodoActions = {

  /**
   * @param  {string} text
   */
  create: function(text) {
    AppDispatcher.dispatch({
      actionType: TodoConstants.TODO_CREATE,
      text: text
    });
  },

  /**
   * @param  {string} id The ID of the TODO item
   * @param  {string} text
   */
  updateText: function(id, text) {
    AppDispatcher.dispatch({
      actionType: TodoConstants.TODO_UPDATE_TEXT,
      id: id,
      text: text
    });
  },

  /**
   * Toggle whether a single TODO is complete
   * @param  {object} todo
   */
```

101

```javascript
  toggleComplete: function(todo) {
    var id = todo.id;
    var actionType = todo.complete ?
        TodoConstants.TODO_UNDO_COMPLETE :
        TodoConstants.TODO_COMPLETE;

    AppDispatcher.dispatch({
      actionType: actionType,
      id: id
    });
  },

  /**
   * Mark all TODOs as complete
   */
  toggleCompleteAll: function() {
    AppDispatcher.dispatch({
      actionType: TodoConstants.TODO_TOGGLE_COMPLETE_ALL
    });
  },

  /**
   * @param  {string} id
   */
  destroy: function(id) {
    AppDispatcher.dispatch({
      actionType: TodoConstants.TODO_DESTROY,
      id: id
    });
  },

  /**
   * Delete all the completed TODOs
   */
  destroyCompleted: function() {
    AppDispatcher.dispatch({
      actionType: TodoConstants.TODO_DESTROY_COMPLETED
    });
  }

};

module.exports = TodoActions;
```

Finally, in Listing 5-10, you encounter the TodoStore.js file, which is the intermediary between the actions, dispatcher, and views. What you see is that each of the events that are processed in the functions in this module are also called from within the callback registry. This registry, which is emboldened in the example that follows, powers all of the delegation between the dispatcher and the views. Each of the functions will do the work that is needed to update the values of the TODOs, after which the method TodoStore.emitChange() is called. This method will tell the React views that it is time to reconcile the views and update the DOM accordingly.

Listing 5-10. TodoStore.js

```javascript
var AppDispatcher = require('../dispatcher/AppDispatcher');
var EventEmitter = require('events').EventEmitter;
var TodoConstants = require('../constants/TodoConstants');
var assign = require('object-assign');

var CHANGE_EVENT = 'change';

var _todos = {};

/**
 * Create a TODO item.
 * @param  {string} text The content of the TODO
 */
function create(text) {
  // Hand waving here -- not showing how this interacts with XHR or persistent
  // server-side storage.
  // Using the current timestamp + random number in place of a real id.
  var id = (+new Date() + Math.floor(Math.random() * 999999)).toString(36);
  _todos[id] = {
    id: id,
    complete: false,
    text: text
  };
}

/**
 * Update a TODO item.
 * @param  {string} id
 * @param {object} updates An object literal containing only the data to be
 *     updated.
 */
function update(id, updates) {
  _todos[id] = assign({}, _todos[id], updates);
}

/**
 * Update all of the TODO items with the same object.
 *     the data to be updated.  Used to mark all TODOs as completed.
 * @param  {object} updates An object literal containing only the data to be
 *     updated.
 */
```

```javascript
function updateAll(updates) {
  for (var id in _todos) {
    update(id, updates);
  }
}

/**
 * Delete a TODO item.
 * @param  {string} id
 */
function destroy(id) {
  delete _todos[id];
}

/**
 * Delete all the completed TODO items.
 */
function destroyCompleted() {
  for (var id in _todos) {
    if (_todos[id].complete) {
      destroy(id);
    }
  }
}

var TodoStore = assign({}, EventEmitter.prototype, {

  /**
   * Tests whether all the remaining TODO items are marked as completed.
   * @return {boolean}
   */
  areAllComplete: function() {
    for (var id in _todos) {
      if (!_todos[id].complete) {
        return false;
      }
    }
    return true;
  },

  /**
   * Get the entire collection of TODOs.
   * @return {object}
   */
  getAll: function() {
    return _todos;
  },
```

```
  emitChange: function() {
    this.emit(CHANGE_EVENT);
  },

  /**
   * @param {function} callback
   */
  addChangeListener: function(callback) {
    this.on(CHANGE_EVENT, callback);
  },

  /**
   * @param {function} callback
   */
  removeChangeListener: function(callback) {
    this.removeListener(CHANGE_EVENT, callback);
  }
});

// Register callback to handle all updates
AppDispatcher.register(function(action) {
  var text;

  switch(action.actionType) {
    case TodoConstants.TODO_CREATE:
      text = action.text.trim();
      if (text !== '') {
        create(text);
        TodoStore.emitChange();
      }
      break;

    case TodoConstants.TODO_TOGGLE_COMPLETE_ALL:
      if (TodoStore.areAllComplete()) {
        updateAll({complete: false});
      } else {
        updateAll({complete: true});
      }
      TodoStore.emitChange();
      break;

    case TodoConstants.TODO_UNDO_COMPLETE:
      update(action.id, {complete: false});
      TodoStore.emitChange();
      break;
```

```
    case TodoConstants.TODO_COMPLETE:
      update(action.id, {complete: true});
      TodoStore.emitChange();
      break;

    case TodoConstants.TODO_UPDATE_TEXT:
      text = action.text.trim();
      if (text !== '') {
        update(action.id, {text: text});
        TodoStore.emitChange();
      }
      break;

    case TodoConstants.TODO_DESTROY:
      destroy(action.id);
      TodoStore.emitChange();
      break;

    case TodoConstants.TODO_DESTROY_COMPLETED:
      destroyCompleted();
      TodoStore.emitChange();
      break;

    default:
      // no op
  }
});

module.exports = TodoStore;
```

Summary

This chapter was a departure from pure React in a way that begins to show you how the React ecosystem works as a whole. Starting with describing how the Flux architecture provides a meaningful and useful mechanism to structure a React application so that it is not only maintainable, but efficiently scalable, you saw how to route your data flow in a single direction to provide the best in class development practices for your React applications. You then took a quick look at the Facebook version of a simple Flux TodoMVC application that showcases how you can begin to structure your React applications in the Flux architected way.

In the following chapter, the last in this introduction to React book, you will dissect a fully functioning Chat application built with React and Flux so that you can get a full understanding of how a complex application can be created in a maintainable and scalable way.

CHAPTER 6

■■■

Using Flux to Structure a React Application

The previous chapter introduced you to the Flux project. Flux represents an efficient application architecture for React applications. You learned the basics of how Flux uses a dispatcher to send actions to the stores, which are then rendered into the DOM using React components. This was all finalized by taking a look at a trivial TodoMVC application that was structured utilizing Flux architecture. In this chapter, you will create a React application that is more involved than the TODO application and structure it according to Flux architecture.

Structuring Your Application

Before you get started creating the components and the Flux architecture for the application you are going to build, you need to define what it is you are going to make. In this example, we'll showcase how data flows in a single direction when you use React and Flux. A great example for that purpose is a Chat application. A Chat application can come in any number of variations, but in this situation the Chat application that you want will look something like the Chat feature in the Facebook interface. You have a list of threads that show that you are communicating with a friend. A messages pane enables you to select a specific thread, follow the history of that thread, and then create new messages. Mocked up, this application might look similar to what is shown in Figure 6-1.

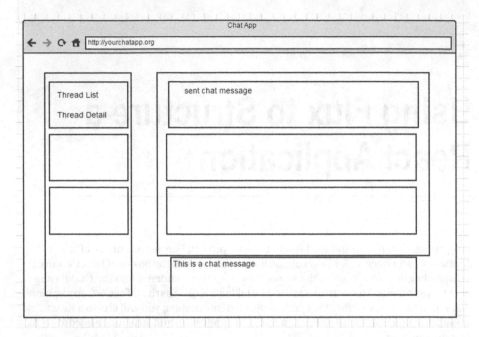

Figure 6-1. *Wireframe of your application*

Looking at the wireframe, you can decipher where you will be able to create React components for your application. The application as a whole will become the parent component. You can then create a message component.

A monolithic message component does not fit the atomic component architecture that you are accustomed to with React, so you need to split the messages portion into three React components. One is for creating the messages, the second is for managing the individual message items in the list, and the third is a container for those message items.

A similar design can be seen when thinking about the message threads on the left side of the wireframe. Here, you will have the threads container and the children of that container are the thread items.

Creating Dispatcher, Stores, Actions, and React Components for the Application

Now that you have a general idea of the application that you are going to create, you could build the React application and utilize whatever mechanism you choose to load the data into the components in order for them to be rendered. This is a valid method, but as you saw in the previous chapter, Flux provides an architecture for React that will make building a Chat application easier than it might be without the use of React and Flux. So now you can start to architect your application utilizing the Flux mindset.

Dispatcher

To start off, you need to create a dispatcher, which as you saw earlier, is just a new instance of the Flux dispatcher module that you can share in your application (Listing 6-1).

Listing 6-1. Dispatcher for the Chat Application

```
var Dispatcher = require('flux').Dispatcher;

module.exports = new Dispatcher();
```

Stores

If you recall, stores in Flux are regarded as a sort of model that you might find in a typical MVC framework, only bigger. Rather than a model representation of a particular element, stores represent a place for all of the data in a logical domain. So, in terms of the Chat application, you can encapsulate all of the message data into a single store, as shown in Listing 6-2.

Listing 6-2. The MessageStore Component

```
var ChatAppDispatcher = require('../dispatcher/ChatAppDispatcher');
var ChatConstants = require('../constants/ChatConstants');
var ChatMessageUtils = require('../utils/ChatMessageUtils');
var EventEmitter = require('events').EventEmitter;
var ThreadStore = require('../stores/ThreadStore');
var assign = require('object-assign');

var ActionTypes = ChatConstants.ActionTypes;
var CHANGE_EVENT = 'change';

var _messages = {};

function _addMessages(rawMessages) {
  rawMessages.forEach(function(message) {
    if (!_messages[message.id]) {
      _messages[message.id] = ChatMessageUtils.convertRawMessage(
        message,
        ThreadStore.getCurrentID()
      );
    }
  });
}
```

```javascript
function _markAllInThreadRead(threadID) {
  for (var id in _messages) {
    if (_messages[id].threadID === threadID) {
      _messages[id].isRead = true;
    }
  }
}

var MessageStore = assign({}, EventEmitter.prototype, {

  emitChange: function() {
    this.emit(CHANGE_EVENT);
  },

  /**
   * @param {function} callback
   */
  addChangeListener: function(callback) {
    this.on(CHANGE_EVENT, callback);
  },

  removeChangeListener: function(callback) {
    this.removeListener(CHANGE_EVENT, callback);
  },

  get: function(id) {
    return _messages[id];
  },

  getAll: function() {
    return _messages;
  },

  /**
   * @param {string} threadID
   */
  getAllForThread: function(threadID) {
    var threadMessages = [];
    for (var id in _messages) {
      if (_messages[id].threadID === threadID) {
        threadMessages.push(_messages[id]);
      }
    }
    threadMessages.sort(function(a, b) {
      if (a.date < b.date) {
        return -1;
```

```
      } else if (a.date > b.date) {
        return 1;
      }
      return 0;
    });
    return threadMessages;
  },

  getAllForCurrentThread: function() {
    return this.getAllForThread(ThreadStore.getCurrentID());
  }

});

MessageStore.dispatchToken = ChatAppDispatcher.register(function(action) {

  switch(action.type) {

    case ActionTypes.CLICK_THREAD:
      ChatAppDispatcher.waitFor([ThreadStore.dispatchToken]);
      _markAllInThreadRead(ThreadStore.getCurrentID());
      MessageStore.emitChange();
      break;

    case ActionTypes.CREATE_MESSAGE:
      var message = ChatMessageUtils.getCreatedMessageData(
        action.text,
        action.currentThreadID
      );
      _messages[message.id] = message;
      MessageStore.emitChange();
      break;

    case ActionTypes.RECEIVE_RAW_MESSAGES:
      _addMessages(action.rawMessages);
      ChatAppDispatcher.waitFor([ThreadStore.dispatchToken]);
      _markAllInThreadRead(ThreadStore.getCurrentID());
      MessageStore.emitChange();
      break;

    default:
      // do nothing
  }

});

module.exports = MessageStore;
```

MessageStore represents all the data for the messages you will be creating or fetching in your Chat application. The first thing that the store must do is register a callback with the dispatcher, which it does with ChatAppDispatcher.register(). That callback becomes the only method to input data into the store. You will see that the callback contains a big switch statement that in this case is keyed off of the different action types that are sent to the callback. Once the applicable case in the switch is encountered, the store will be able to do something with the action and can then send emitChange(), which will then communicate to the views that they can then fetch the new data from the stores.

It is noteworthy to see that the store does not contain any public method to set the data, meaning everything is accessed through getters. This means you don't have to worry about data leaking into your store from another part of the application. This makes the store a literal storage bin for your data. It will be able to take care of your messages and update them via the dispatcher callback, and then notify you of changes. This can be seen in MessageStore, where the actionType is ActionTypes.RECEIVE_RAW_MESSAGES. Once this is received, MessageStore will add the messages via its private _addMessages function, mark the messages in that thread as read, and finally emit the changes via EventEmitter.

Now that you have seen MessageStore, you need to be able to control which threads you have available to you in your Chat application. This is done with ThreadStore (Listing 6-3).

Listing 6-3. The ThreadStore Component

```
var ChatAppDispatcher = require('../dispatcher/ChatAppDispatcher');
var ChatConstants = require('../constants/ChatConstants');
var ChatMessageUtils = require('../utils/ChatMessageUtils');
var EventEmitter = require('events').EventEmitter;
var assign = require('object-assign');

var ActionTypes = ChatConstants.ActionTypes;
var CHANGE_EVENT = 'change';

var _currentID = null;
var _threads = {};

var ThreadStore = assign({}, EventEmitter.prototype, {

init: function(rawMessages) {
  rawMessages.forEach(function(message) {
    var threadID = message.threadID;
    var thread = _threads[threadID];

    if (!(thread && thread.lastTimestamp > message.timestamp)) {
      _threads[threadID] = {
        id: threadID,
        name: message.threadName,
        lastMessage: ChatMessageUtils.convertRawMessage(message, _currentID)
      };
    }
  }, this);
```

```
  if (!_currentID) {
    var allChrono = this.getAllChrono();
    _currentID = allChrono[allChrono.length - 1].id;
  }
  _threads[_currentID].lastMessage.isRead = true;
},
emitChange: function() {
  this.emit(CHANGE_EVENT);
},

/**
 * @param {function} callback
 */
addChangeListener: function(callback) {
  this.on(CHANGE_EVENT, callback);
},

/**
 * @param {function} callback
 */
removeChangeListener: function(callback) {
  this.removeListener(CHANGE_EVENT, callback);
},

/**
 * @param {string} id
 */
get: function(id) {
  return _threads[id];
},

getAll: function() {
  return _threads;
},

getAllChrono: function() {
  var orderedThreads = [];
  for (var id in _threads) {
    var thread = _threads[id];
    orderedThreads.push(thread);
  }
  orderedThreads.sort(function(a, b) {
    if (a.lastMessage.date < b.lastMessage.date) {
      return -1;
    } else if (a.lastMessage.date > b.lastMessage.date) {
      return 1;
    }
```

113

```
      return 0;
    });
    return orderedThreads;
  },

  getCurrentID: function() {
    return _currentID;
  },

  getCurrent: function() {
    return this.get(this.getCurrentID());
  }

});

ThreadStore.dispatchToken = ChatAppDispatcher.register(function(action) {

  switch(action.type) {

    case ActionTypes.CLICK_THREAD:
      _currentID = action.threadID;
      _threads[_currentID].lastMessage.isRead = true;
      ThreadStore.emitChange();
      break;

    case ActionTypes.RECEIVE_RAW_MESSAGES:
      ThreadStore.init(action.rawMessages);
      ThreadStore.emitChange();
      break;

    default:
      // do nothing
  }

});

module.exports = ThreadStore;
```

ThreadStore, just like MessageStore, has only public getter methods and no setter methods. ThreadStore registers a callback with the dispatcher, which contains the switch statement that will control how the store reacts to the actions that are sent via the dispatcher. The switch statements respond to the particular ActionTypes sent via the dispatcher and then send the emitChange() event.

Related to ThreadStore is UnreadThreadStore (Listing 6-4). This store will be referenced in the ThreadSection component and bound to the _onChange event. This way the component can update the state when the threads are marked as unread.

Listing 6-4. The UnreadThreadStore Component

```
var ChatAppDispatcher = require('../dispatcher/ChatAppDispatcher');
var ChatConstants = require('../constants/ChatConstants');
var EventEmitter = require('events').EventEmitter;
var MessageStore = require('../stores/MessageStore');
var ThreadStore = require('../stores/ThreadStore');
var assign = require('object-assign');

var ActionTypes = ChatConstants.ActionTypes;
var CHANGE_EVENT = 'change';

var UnreadThreadStore = assign({}, EventEmitter.prototype, {

  emitChange: function() {
    this.emit(CHANGE_EVENT);
  },

  /**
   * @param {function} callback
   */
  addChangeListener: function(callback) {
    this.on(CHANGE_EVENT, callback);
  },

  /**
   * @param {function} callback
   */
  removeChangeListener: function(callback) {
    this.removeListener(CHANGE_EVENT, callback);
  },

  getCount: function() {
    var threads = ThreadStore.getAll();
    var unreadCount = 0;
    for (var id in threads) {
      if (!threads[id].lastMessage.isRead) {
        unreadCount++;
      }
    }
    return unreadCount;
  }

});
```

```
UnreadThreadStore.dispatchToken = ChatAppDispatcher.register(function(action) {
  ChatAppDispatcher.waitFor([
    ThreadStore.dispatchToken,
    MessageStore.dispatchToken
  ]);

  switch (action.type) {

    case ActionTypes.CLICK_THREAD:
      UnreadThreadStore.emitChange();
      break;

    case ActionTypes.RECEIVE_RAW_MESSAGES:
      UnreadThreadStore.emitChange();
      break;

    default:
      // do nothing
  }
});

module.exports = UnreadThreadStore;
```

That is it for the stores. They get data from the dispatcher in the form of an object literal via a registered callback and then emit events. Next you will examine the actions, or in this case the action creators, that will be invoked from your React views.

Actions

Actions drive the one-way data flow of your Flux Chat application. Without the actions, the views will not receive updates from the stores because nothing is passed to the dispatcher to call the stores' callbacks. The actions in this example are in the form of action creators. These creators can create an action from React's views or you can get a message from a WebAPI on your server. In Listing 6-5, you will not need to create a server to serve Chat requests, but the following code snippet highlights how you might create a ServerAction. This exports some methods that would fetch, or retrieve, the data from your server and then dispatch that data to the Flux application via the .dispatch() function.

Listing 6-5. This ServerActionCreator Can Receive Messages from an API and Dispatch to the Rest of the Flux Application

```
var ChatAppDispatcher = require('../dispatcher/ChatAppDispatcher');
var ChatConstants = require('../constants/ChatConstants');

var ActionTypes = ChatConstants.ActionTypes;
```

```
module.exports = {

  receiveAll: function(rawMessages) {
    ChatAppDispatcher.dispatch({
      type: ActionTypes.RECEIVE_RAW_MESSAGES,
      rawMessages: rawMessages
    });
  },

  receiveCreatedMessage: function(createdMessage) {
    ChatAppDispatcher.dispatch({
      type: ActionTypes.RECEIVE_RAW_CREATED_MESSAGE,
      rawMessage: createdMessage
    });
  }

};
```

Another functionality of action creators is that they can become a utility to pass information from the views to the server and the dispatcher. This is precisely what happens with MessageAction in this Flux example (Listing 6-6). The MessageComposer component, which you will see in the next section, calls MessageAction to create a message. This will first send the message data to the dispatcher, and also call the API utilities that you have in your application to update the data on the server, as shown in Listing 6-6.

Listing 6-6. The MessageActionCreator Will Dispatch Message Data via the Dispatcher and Update the Server via an API Method

```
var ChatAppDispatcher = require('../dispatcher/ChatAppDispatcher');
var ChatConstants = require('../constants/ChatConstants');
var ChatWebAPIUtils = require('../utils/ChatWebAPIUtils');
var ChatMessageUtils = require('../utils/ChatMessageUtils');

var ActionTypes = ChatConstants.ActionTypes;

module.exports = {

  createMessage: function(text, currentThreadID) {
    ChatAppDispatcher.dispatch({
      type: ActionTypes.CREATE_MESSAGE,
      text: text,
      currentThreadID: currentThreadID
    });
    var message = ChatMessageUtils.getCreatedMessageData(text,
    currentThreadID);
    ChatWebAPIUtils.createMessage(message);
  }

};
```

In your Chat application, the only remaining action to account for is what happens when someone clicks a thread. This action is handled by the ThreadActionCreator, which is shown in Listing 6-7.

Listing 6-7. ThreadActionCreator Verifies that the Thread of a Given ID Has Been Clicked in the Application

```
var ChatAppDispatcher = require('../dispatcher/ChatAppDispatcher');
var ChatConstants = require('../constants/ChatConstants');

var ActionTypes = ChatConstants.ActionTypes;

module.exports = {

  clickThread: function(threadID) {
    ChatAppDispatcher.dispatch({
      type: ActionTypes.CLICK_THREAD,
      threadID: threadID
    });
  }

};
```

React Components

The React components are not dissimilar from what you have previously seen in this book; however, they do involve utilizing the state more aggressively to account for the Chat application and its Flux architecture. Let's start by creating the ThreadSection component. In order to that, you will need to create the ThreadListItem (Listing 6-8), which will be added during the render() process of the ThreadSection. The ThreadListItem also calls ThreadAction for ThreadClick to send the event to the dispatcher.

Listing 6-8. ThreadListItem—Note the _onClick Binding to the ThreadAction for clickThread

```
var ChatThreadActionCreators = require('../actions/
ChatThreadActionCreators');
var React = require('react');
// Note: cx will be obsolete soon so you can use
// https://github.com/JedWatson/classnames as a replacement
var cx = require('react/lib/cx');

var ReactPropTypes = React.PropTypes;
```

```
var ThreadListItem = React.createClass({

  propTypes: {
    thread: ReactPropTypes.object,
    currentThreadID: ReactPropTypes.string
  },

  render: function() {
    var thread = this.props.thread;
    var lastMessage = thread.lastMessage;
    return (
      <li
        className={cx({
          'thread-list-item': true,
          'active': thread.id === this.props.currentThreadID
        })}
        onClick={this._onClick}>
        <h5 className="thread-name">{thread.name}</h5>
        <div className="thread-time">
          {lastMessage.date.toLocaleTimeString()}
        </div>
        <div className="thread-last-message">
          {lastMessage.text}
        </div>
      </li>
    );
  },

  _onClick: function() {
    ChatThreadActionCreators.clickThread(this.props.thread.id);
  }

});

module.exports = ThreadListItem;
```

■ **Note**   The cx component is being deprecated, but a standalone for class manipulation can be found at https://github.com/JedWatson/classnames. If you choose to utilize this sort of class manipulation, you can also find a solution at http:// reactcss.com.

Now that you have the ThreadListItems, you can gather these into your ThreadSection, as shown in Listing 6-9. This ThreadSection fetches the threads from ThreadStore and UnreadThreadStore during the component's lifecycle event called getInitialState. This will then set the state to control how many ThreadListItems are created in the render function.

Listing 6-9. The ThreadSection Component

```
var React = require('react');
var MessageStore = require('../stores/MessageStore');
var ThreadListItem = require('../components/ThreadListItem.react');
var ThreadStore = require('../stores/ThreadStore');
var UnreadThreadStore = require('../stores/UnreadThreadStore');

function getStateFromStores() {
  return {
    threads: ThreadStore.getAllChrono(),
    currentThreadID: ThreadStore.getCurrentID(),
    unreadCount: UnreadThreadStore.getCount()
  };
}

var ThreadSection = React.createClass({

  getInitialState: function() {
    return getStateFromStores();
  },

  componentDidMount: function() {
    ThreadStore.addChangeListener(this._onChange);
    UnreadThreadStore.addChangeListener(this._onChange);
  },

  componentWillUnmount: function() {
    ThreadStore.removeChangeListener(this._onChange);
    UnreadThreadStore.removeChangeListener(this._onChange);
  },

  render: function() {
    var threadListItems = this.state.threads.map(function(thread) {
      return (
        <ThreadListItem
          key={thread.id}
          thread={thread}
          currentThreadID={this.state.currentThreadID}
        />
      );
    }, this);
    var unread =
      this.state.unreadCount === 0 ?
      null :
      <span>Unread threads: {this.state.unreadCount}</span>;
```

```
    return (
      <div className="thread-section">
        <div className="thread-count">
          {unread}
        </div>
        <ul className="thread-list">
          {threadListItems}
        </ul>
      </div>
    );
  },

  /**
   * Event handler for 'change' events coming from the stores
   */
  _onChange: function() {
    this.setState(getStateFromStores());
  }

});

module.exports = ThreadSection;
```

You have now used React and Flux to create the thread section of your application. The MessageSection is next and it requires that you create a MessageListItem component as well as a MessageComposer component, as shown in Listing 6-10.

Listing 6-10. MessageComposer—Binds to the Textarea and Sends the Text to the MessageActionCreators

```
var ChatMessageActionCreators = require('../actions/
ChatMessageActionCreators');
var React = require('react');

var ENTER_KEY_CODE = 13;

var MessageComposer = React.createClass({

  propTypes: {
    threadID: React.PropTypes.string.isRequired
  },

  getInitialState: function() {
    return {text: ''};
  },
```

```
  render: function() {
    return (
      <textarea
        className="message-composer"
        name="message"
        value={this.state.text}
        onChange={this._onChange}
        onKeyDown={this._onKeyDown}
      />
    );
  },

  _onChange: function(event, value) {
    this.setState({text: event.target.value});
  },

  _onKeyDown: function(event) {
    if (event.keyCode === ENTER_KEY_CODE) {
      event.preventDefault();
      var text = this.state.text.trim();
      if (text) {
        ChatMessageActionCreators.createMessage(text, this.props.threadID);
      }
      this.setState({text: ''});
    }
  }
});

module.exports = MessageComposer;
```

The MessageComposer component is a textarea that will bind its change
event to the state.text and keydown events. The keydown event will look for the
Enter key on the keyboard. If it has been pressed, MessageComposer will call the
ChatMessageActionCreators.createMessage() function to create the action to send to
the API server and the dispatcher.

MessageListItems (Listing 6-11) is just an HTML list item that contains the message
data that is passed to it from MessageSection.

Listing 6-11. MessageListItems Contain Message Details

```
var React = require('react');

var ReactPropTypes = React.PropTypes;

var MessageListItem = React.createClass({

  propTypes: {
    message: ReactPropTypes.object
  },
```

```
render: function() {
  var message = this.props.message;
  return (
    <li className="message-list-item">
      <h5 className="message-author-name">{message.authorName}</h5>
      <div className="message-time">
        {message.date.toLocaleTmeString()}
      </div>
      <div className="message-text">{message.text}</div>
    </li>
  );
}

});

module.exports = MessageListItem;
```

The MessageSection in Listing 6-12 first fetches the state from the stores via the getInitialState React lifecycle. This fetches the current thread and gets its messages. Once the component mounts, in componentDidMount, MessageStore and ThreadStore both bind listeners to the _onChange event. This change event this.setState(getState FromStores()); is called again, just as if the initial state is set. This is the quintessential takeaway from both React and Flux. It's a single directional data flow in which every render comes from the fetch of state from the stores, and only one method to update the stores. MessageSection also aggregates the messages added to the state object and creates new MessageListItems for each message.

Listing 6-12. The MessageSection Component

```
var MessageComposer = require('./MessageComposer.react');
var MessageListItem = require('./MessageListItem.react');
var MessageStore = require('../stores/MessageStore');
var React = require('react');
var ThreadStore = require('../stores/ThreadStore');

function getStateFromStores() {
  return {
    messages: MessageStore.getAllForCurrentThread(),
    thread: ThreadStore.getCurrent()
  };
}

function getMessageListItem(message) {
  return (
    <MessageListItem
      key={message.id}
      message={message}
    />
  );
}
```

123

```
var MessageSection = React.createClass({

  getInitialState: function() {
    return getStateFromStores();
  },

  componentDidMount: function() {
    this._scrollToBottom();
    MessageStore.addChangeListener(this._onChange);
    ThreadStore.addChangeListener(this._onChange);
  },

  componentWillUnmount: function() {
    MessageStore.removeChangeListener(this._onChange);
    ThreadStore.removeChangeListener(this._onChange);
  },

  render: function() {
    var messageListItems = this.state.messages.map(getMessageListItem);
    return (
      <div className="message-section">
        <h3 className="message-thread-heading">{this.state.thread.name}</h3>
        <ul className="message-list" ref="messageList">
          {messageListItems}
        </ul>
        <MessageComposer threadID={this.state.thread.id}/>
      </div>
    );
  },

  componentDidUpdate: function() {
    this._scrollToBottom();
  },

  _scrollToBottom: function() {
    var ul = this.refs.messageList.getDOMNode();
    ul.scrollTop = ul.scrollHeight;
  },

  /**
   * Event handler for 'change' events coming from the MessageStore
   */
  _onChange: function() {
    this.setState(getStateFromStores());
  }

});

module.exports = MessageSection;
```

You now have the completed MessageSection and ThreadSection of the application. The only remaining item is to put these all together in the ChatApp component shown in Listing 6-13.

Listing 6-13. The ChatApp Component

```
var MessageSection = require('./MessageSection.react');
var React = require('react');
var ThreadSection = require('./ThreadSection.react');

var ChatApp = React.createClass({

  render: function() {
    return (
      <div className="chatapp">
        <ThreadSection />
        <MessageSection />
      </div>
    );
  }

});

module.exports = ChatApp;
```

Writing Tests

As you saw earlier in the book, Jest is a useful tool for writing tests. Listing 6-14 is a simple test that you can use as a model. This test is written for UnreadThreadStore, and it ensures that there is a proper count of unread threads. It also ensures that the callback is registered with the dispatcher.

Listing 6-14. UnreadThreadCount Tests

```
jest.dontMock('../UnreadThreadStore');
jest.dontMock('object-assign');

describe('UnreadThreadStore', function() {

  var ChatAppDispatcher;
  var UnreadThreadStore;
  var callback;

  beforeEach(function() {
    ChatAppDispatcher = require('../../dispatcher/ChatAppDispatcher');
    UnreadThreadStore = require('../UnreadThreadStore');
    callback = ChatAppDispatcher.register.mock.calls[0][0];
  });
```

```
it('registers a callback with the dispatcher', function() {
  expect(ChatAppDispatcher.register.mock.calls.length).toBe(1);
});

it('provides the unread thread count', function() {
  var ThreadStore = require('../ThreadStore');
  ThreadStore.getAll.mockReturnValueOnce(
    {
      foo: {lastMessage: {isRead: false}},
      bar: {lastMessage: {isRead: false}},
      baz: {lastMessage: {isRead: true}}
    }
  );
  expect(UnreadThreadStore.getCount()).toBe(2);
});

});
```

Running the Application

You can run this application from the root of the repository found at https://github.com/cgack/flux/tree/master/examples/flux-chat. Once you have cloned the repository, or the parent of that fork, you can run npm install from the flux-chat directory. This will pull down all the needed dependencies. After that, simply run npm test to run the tests.

To finally run the application, use the npm start command. Doing so will start the watcher and convert all of the app.js bootstrap code to the bundle.js file. You then just need to navigate your browser to the index.html file to see the Chat application in action.

Summary

In this chapter, you saw a more contrived example of how React and Flux work together. This example showed more React components and uses of the state and illustrated a single directional data flow. This example is a great jumping-off point to start building your own great React components and applications, with or without Flux.

This book set out to introduce you to React and get you accustomed to seeing web development through the lens of React's components. I hope that you have enjoyed the book and found it useful.

Index

Get the eBook for only $5!

Why limit yourself?

Now you can take the weightless companion with you wherever you go and access your content on your PC, phone, tablet, or reader.

Since you've purchased this print book, we're happy to offer you the eBook in all 3 formats for just $5.

Convenient and fully searchable, the PDF version enables you to easily find and copy code—or perform examples by quickly toggling between instructions and applications. The MOBI format is ideal for your Kindle, while the ePUB can be utilized on a variety of mobile devices.

To learn more, go to www.apress.com/companion or contact support@apress.com.

Printed in the United States
By Bookmasters